HAHAHAHAHAHAHAHAHEEHEEHEEHEE! I pick up a fat lady, sh— shirt says, "Eat right, exercise, die anyway—why not pig out?" HAHAHAHAHAHA! She was huge—I had to pull her out of the ba— HAHAHAHAHA! Oh there go Chinese cabdriver—they're wimps— this! HAHAHAHAHAHA! You know, this is the church where Jo— and Marilyn Monroe were married.

Once we got out of the cab, the initial shock dissolved into simple of the most bizarre and entertaining cab ride we had ever experie— laughter built and crescendoed, and we fell into benches in Washin— to recover. It sounded something like this—HAHAHAHAHAHA!

Scrapbooks To Cherish

Telling your most
heartfelt stories

Simple Scrapbooks

Scrapbooks to Cherish

Simple Scrapbooks Magazine
14850 Pony Express Road
Bluffdale, UT 84065
www.simplescrapbooksmag.com

Primedia Enthusiast Media
200 Madison Avenue, 8th Floor
New York, NY 10016-3906

Printed in Korea
ISBN 1-929180-86-1

For Simple Scrapbooks

Founding Editor . . . . Stacy Julian

Editor in Chief . . . . Lin Sorenson

Special Projects Editor . . . . . Lynda Angelastro

Managing Editor . . . . Angie Lucas

Creative Editor . . . . Wendy Smedley

Editorial Board . . . . Tara Cowper

Darci Dowdle

Donna Downey

Deanna Lambson

Kris Parkin

Renee Pearson

Kathleen Samuelson

Cathy Zielske

Associate Editors . . . . Elisha Snow

Mark Zoellner

Editorial Assistants . . . . Allison Barnes

Mary Ruth Francks

Carolyn Jolley

Art Director . . . . Don Lambson

Senior Designer . . . . John Youngberg

Book and Cover Design

Daniel Ruesch Design

Photography

John Luke Photography

Table of Contents

At the risk of sounding trite, I'm not sure I can find the words to describe how **Scrapbooks to Cherish** and the albums it honors makes me feel.

When it came time to select "winners" in our Coolest Album Ever contest, I flew to Utah to spend the day with three other editors. We met in Wendy Smedley's home so we could be removed from the bustle of the office and immerse ourselves in the stories of dozens of album finalists. We sat on the floor for hours laughing and crying. Over and over we exclaimed, "I've got to read you this!" or "Just look at this one!" and "They get it, they really get it!" The experience was one I won't soon forget.

Boarding the plane home that night, I sat back, closed my eyes and let the day's emotions wash over me. Tears came again—but this time as a result of deep appreciation for the opportunity to be part of Simple Scrapbooks. Our mission is to encourage people to look beyond their piles of photos long enough to connect to and share their defining moments and most meaningful memories. I realized that day that we are succeeding, one album at a time. The message of "simplify" is making a difference.

I don't have to search for just the right words to describe the meaning these albums hold, because I'm convinced that as you read and absorb them yourself, you'll understand their significance. More than anything we've published, this book embodies what we are about. And so, I dedicate it to all of the women who entered this contest and created a *scrapbook to cherish*—you are all winners.

With my heart and soul,

Stacy Julian

Stacy Julian
Founding Editor
Simple Scrapbooks

Introduction

"If you would not be
forgotten as soon as
you are dead,
either write things
worth reading
or do things worth
writing."

BENJAMIN FRANKLIN

Simple Scrapbooks' "Coolest Album Ever" Contest

For our first "Coolest Album Ever" contest, we issued a call to our readers to make an album about an aspect of their lives that has defined or changed them.

Entries poured into our offices, and we were suddenly faced with the awesome responsibility of judging them. There were stories of weddings, family reunions and vacations; heart-wrenching accounts of loss and triumph; and amazing chronicles of the connections between people, places and history. The albums were all sizes and shapes; some featured sections with dozens of layouts, while others were only a few pages long. Each was a unique expression of its creator.

Each entry included a completed Formula Worksheet, found in every issue of *Simple Scrapbooks* magazine. The Formula Worksheet is a fill-in-the-blank guide featuring nine questions that help you determine the purpose, format and preparation of a theme album. The backside of the worksheet is left blank for sketches, paper swatches and checklists. Using the Formula Worksheet helps you simplify the creative processes of building a scrapbook.

The worksheet also helped our editorial team better understand the goals of each designer who entered the contest. Much like going backstage after a play, we were afforded a more in depth look at the inner workings of each album—why color schemes were chosen, what design decisions were made to contribute to a unified presentation, and what photos and information had to be located with the help of friends or family members.

Clearly evident was the thought and emotion that went into each and every entry.

Formula Worksheet: A Formula Worksheet for your use can be found at the end of this book. The worksheet is also bound into every copy of *Simple Scrapbooks* magazine, and located online at www.simplescrapbooksmag.com/download.

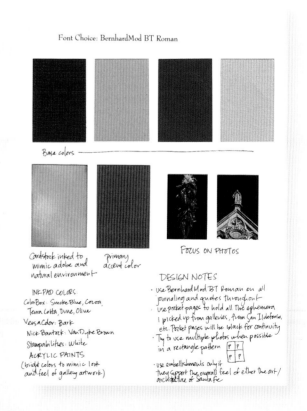

Here is a brief description of our contest's five categories:

Tributes

The story of a person, place or thing that you love (the emphasis is on the topic, not your relationship to it). For example, you may pay tribute to your Grandmother's life, your hometown or a beloved collection.

Celebrations

Shares the significance of special days and milestone events, from birthday parties and weddings to time-honored holiday traditions.

Self Discovery

An exploration of your life, a personal journey or life-changing experience; or a hobby, challenge or triumph and how it affected you.

Relationships

Explores your association with and connection to someone you love—for example, your feelings about your sister, what she means to you and how she influences your life; or the bond you share with a special friend or pet.

Journey

Shares the account of a trip or vacation you've taken, including the sights, experiences and events that made this journey memorable.

How To Use This Book

This book is different from most scrapbook idea books—for one main reason. It begs to be savored, not just glanced through. This is a curl-up-in-a-blanket-with-a-warm-cup-of-tea kind of book. We want you to feel you are personally viewing each winning album; therefore all the journaling is readable and a note from each album's creator accompanies every project. Many albums show every page and you'll be reading the actual story, not our report of it. Don't rush when reading these albums; rather, take time to appreciate each one.

Consider the themes and ideas presented, those from the album designers and the ones that surface from your own memory as you read. We're sure you'll find elements in these projects that you'll love and want to copy, and this is good! While noting these instant ideas, hold out also for the personal inspiration that comes from a quiet, careful and more studied reflection.

Scrapbooking is a fun, creative outlet, but it's also a chance to compile something meaningful—something that you and those you love will cherish for a very long time.

To this end we wish you happy reading!

CHAPTER ONE

· · · · · · · · · · · · · · ·

Tributes

*"It is extraordinary
how extraordinary the
ordinary person is."*

GEORGE F. WILL

Tribute albums are a wonderful way to honor family heritage, a friend, family member, pet, place or organization that has meaning for you. The albums featured in this chapter of **Scrapbooks to Cherish** were the most original entries in our contest. Our winners scrapbooked their tributes using the unique frames of home, quilts, heritage language and even a popular board game.

You'll love what **Beth Proudfoot** has hanging on the wall in her entryway.

Yes, it's a scrapbook. A scrapbook housed in an old-style wall mailbox. The album is there to preserve the memories of all who have lived in the house. We thought this was a wonderful and meaningful idea, and you will too when you see it.

Houses aren't the only original scrapbook ideas we received in the tribute category. **Angie Hunt's** album pays tribute to her family via their

language heritage. Read about these unique expressions, and see photos of the family members who used them, in her fascinating album.

Lori Robb's album is a game of Clue. The object is to use the clues left in each "room" to try and guess who the book is about. On the last page, we discover the book is a tribute to Lori's teenage daughter who is, of course, crazy about the game Clue.

Lisa Moorefield's tribute album is a loving look at family and heritage through photos and stories of the family's quilt collection.

Let's open the innovative and creative albums of our Tribute winners and learn from them as they surround themselves with history, language, games and love.

"This is a tribute album. Not a tribute to a house, as it may appear to be at first glance. It's much more than that. You see, it's a tribute to the people, the families, who have filled this house with their laughter and their love; the people who have made this house a home. Although my house is almost eighty years old, I know all of these people. I know their names. I know their stories. Most importantly, I know that they were not so different from my own family. I had to preserve these stories, this connection, not only for our two families, but for the families who will live here in another eighty years. This album connects people; it connects the past, the present and the future. Now that is cool."

This album is intended to stay here. It belongs here so that the stories of the Starnar and Proudfoot families will live within the walls of this home. It belongs here so that more families who will one day love and laugh and live here can add their stories. This home transcends time. It connects the past, the present, and the future. This home connects us.

Frank and Ruth Starnar built their dream home in 1925, for $6,000 and raised their two daughters there. Members of the Starnar family lived in the Center Street house continuously for more than 75 years.

If you've ever wondered about the people who lived in your home before you did, you'll love Beth Proudfoot's album "Within These Walls." Beth lives in an older home with a rich history. She wanted to honor and preserve that history by documenting the generations, including her own family, who have lived in the home. She wanted people who live in or visit the home to know the stories of the home's occupants, past and present. The album, with its mailbox container, was designed to be displayed inside the house, and to be a legacy that stays with the home, no matter who is living there.

arnars paid
ouse built.

Within These Walls

Beth's Approach

Beth used an old-fashioned mailbox to house and display the scrapbook she made about the people who've lived in her house. The mailbox hangs in a place of honor in the entry of Beth's home and is a natural conversation starter.

Beth has taken a simple scrapbook album and made it the heart of her home. It is beautiful, inspirational and accessible.

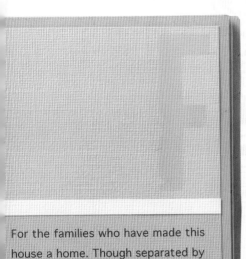

← **Tag Journaling:** Back in 1925, the Starnars paid $6,000 to have this house built.

For the families who have made this house a home. Though separated by more than seventy years, we are all similar; in our values, in our hopes, and in our everyday lives. This home transcends time. It connects the past, the present, and the future. This home connects us.

Tag Journaling: Janice Butler Starnar was a nurse. She married and had children. Mary Louise Starnar was a schoolteacher. She lived in the house for 73 years. She was raised here, cared for her ailing parents here, and grew old here. She married Ellwood Thornton, her sister's widower, at the age of 75. A year later, she sold the house to us.

↓

a nurse. She married uise Starnar was a school ouse for 73 years. She her ailing parents here, rried Ellwood Thornton, e age of 75. A year later

Mary Louise and Janice (pictured in 1932) were toddlers when this house was built. As Mary Louise recalls, "We enjoyed rollerskating and bicycle riding. We explored and roamed the vacant fields around us. We picked wild flowers and strawberries and caught lightning bugs. We sometimes played croquet."

enter Street knew each
le had lived here several
could be seen sitting on
e weather was good in
it was a quieter and more

Mary Louise Starnar

2001 for $275,000.
tember 11th and
bility and security.

For Kevin and I (pictured in 2004), everything is encompassed within the walls of
this house: our identity, our dreams, our
love, and our memories. Christmas day,
Jack's first day of school, Sam's first day
home from the hospital; these are the
moments here that I'll always remember.

↑ **Tag Journaling:** We bought this house in 2001 for
$275,000. It was four days after September 11th and
we were grasping for stability and security.

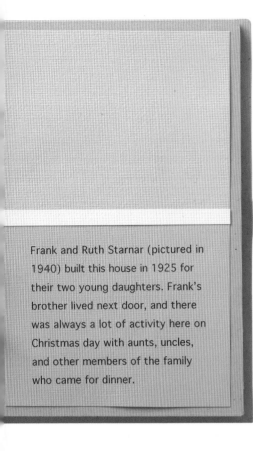

Frank and Ruth Starnar (pictured in 1940) built this house in 1925 for their two young daughters. Frank's brother lived next door, and there was always a lot of activity here on Christmas day with aunts, uncles, and other members of the family who came for dinner.

← **Tag Journaling:** "Back then, everyone on Center Street knew each other and most of the people had lived here several years. Many of the women could be seen sitting on their front porches when the weather was good in the afternoon. On the whole, it was a quieter and more leisurely lifestyle." *Mary Louise Starnar*

Tag Journaling: Before moving in, we spent six weeks renovating the house. The kitchen and bathroom was remodeled, the floors were refinished, and every wall was repainted.

↓

nt six weeks renovating
d bathroom was remodeled,
, and every wall was

Jack and Sam (pictured in 2004) make this house come alive with their laughter and their love for one another. Almost eighty years later, they are doing the same things that Mary Louise and Janice did as sisters: riding bikes, catching fireflies and playing croquet (with some baseball thrown in for good measure).

"I am submitting 'In Our Own Words' in the tribute category of the 'My Coolest Album Ever' contest because it is my tribute to the words and expressions that are part of my family's language heritage. It has been a rewarding project. It has proven to be a great conversation piece and has sparked enjoyable reminiscences with family members and other contributors."

WRITER IN RESIDENCE

Too Precious To Store Away
HEIRLOOM LANGUAGE

By Jan Karon

Just as she collects heirloom linens and silver, novelist Jan Karon treasures the sayings of her grandmother, Fannie Belle Bush Cloer (1883–1993), keeping her spirit — and her spirited past — alive.

Angie Hunt grew up betwixt-n-between Gray and Macon, Georgia, on the Lite-N-Tie Road. Supposedly the road got its name from an era when you might "lite" from your horse and tie him to a hitching post.

"In Our Own Words" is the tangible and meaningful way Angie chose to pay tribute to the speech patterns and unique sayings of her family. An article in *Victoria* magazine first sparked her interest in preserving her family's way of speaking. After reading the article she realized that preserving her family's unique 'voice' was as important as preserving family photos, traditions and stories. Angie's focus on her linguistic inheritance, and the ancestors and family members who have handed that legacy down to her, made it truly her "Coolest Album Ever."

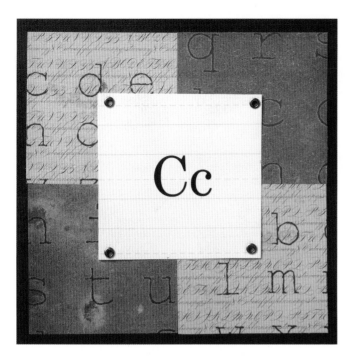

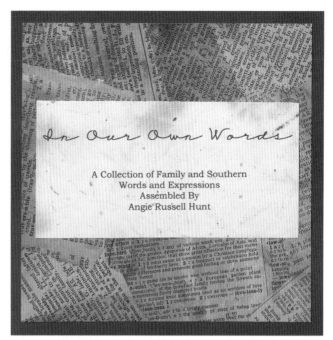

In Our Own Words

A Collection of Family and Southern
Words and Expressions
Assembled By
Angie Russell Hunt

Cuttin' A Fool

Acting or cutting up, creating a disturbance, or being loud, showy, or disruptive. (Synonymous with Actin' A Fool, Raisin' Caine, Raisin' A Fuss, Raisin' A Ruckus, or Raisin' Sand.)

Joe Brown (l) and Jack Hoover (r) are just cuttin' a fool while Uncle Buddy, Gram's brother Lonnie, (far r) stands by and watches them cut up.

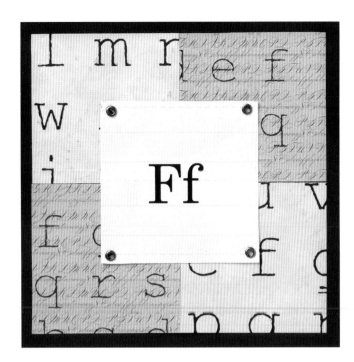

Angie's Approach

The magazine article that inspired Angie suggested she reflect on, and compile, a list of expressions common to her family's regional dialect. At the planning stage, Angie discovered that the list was much longer than she had expected. Many of the words and phrases she once considered commonplace were, she realized, very regional. She searched for a way of organizing these many expressions and decided that a picture dictionary would be both interesting and meaningful. This approach also allowed Angie to showcase favorite family photos that had previously seemed random and difficult to place in other albums.

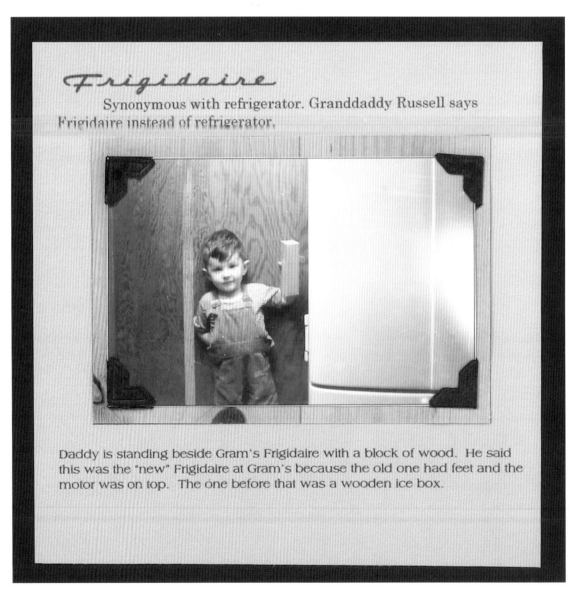

Frigidaire
Synonymous with refrigerator. Granddaddy Russell says Frigidaire instead of refrigerator.

Daddy is standing beside Gram's Frigidaire with a block of wood. He said this was the "new" Frigidaire at Gram's because the old one had feet and the motor was on top. The one before that was a wooden ice box.

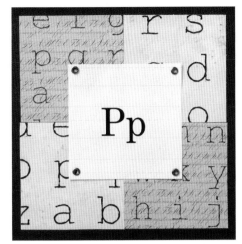

Pitcher

A container for iced tea, lemonade, etc.; or a photograph.

Aunt Elizabeth (or Liba, as everyone calls her) holds a "pitcher" of Uncle James while she awaits his return from his tour of duty in WWII. Uncle James served in the Army from 1942-1945. He was a staff sargeant assigned to the Army Air Corps in the European Theatre of Operations.

Play Purty

Can be a verb meaning to play nice or to behave or a noun that means a toy.

With a little creativity, ordinary items also served as play purties in place of store-bought toys. For Daddy, the water hose was a fun and practical play purty when it was hot. When Sherry and I spent the night with Grandma, Merle Norman bottles were play purties in the tub.

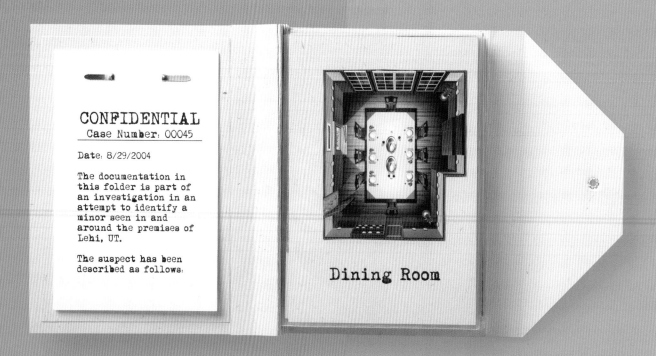

CONFIDENTIAL
Case Number: 00045

Date: 8/29/2004

The documentation in
this folder is part of
an investigation in an
attempt to identify a
minor seen in and
around the premises of
Lehi, UT.

The suspect has been
described as follows:

Dining Room

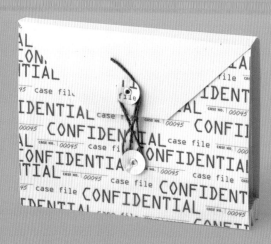

"My daughter loves the game Clue, so when I saw the Clue patterned paper at the scrapbook store, I knew I had to do something for her. She has been begging me for a while to do a scrapbook just about her. So I did. I prefer to do very non-traditional 'About Me' type of scrapbooks, and this is my "Coolest Album Ever."'

So who *did* leave Harry Potter, Lois Duncan and different types of mystery and adventure books scattered all over the Library?

Find out all kinds of interesting things in Lori's project, a joyful and light-hearted—but meaningful—tribute to her daughter through Chandra's love of the game of Clue. On each "room" page, we discover details of her talented daughter's life and accomplishments.

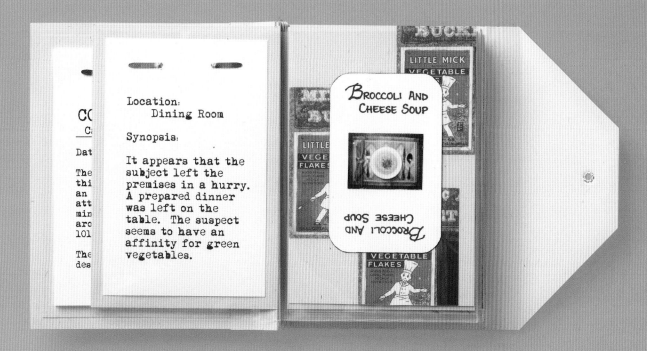

Location:
Dining Room

Synopsis:

It appears that the subject left the premises in a hurry. A prepared dinner was left on the table. The suspect seems to have an affinity for green vegetables.

Broccoli And Cheese Soup

Billiard Room

Lori tried to remain faithful to the Clue game while designing the pages. The intro page asks, "Who is the suspect?" The reader "enters a room" before turning the page to see the associated "clue card" page, and the closing page "opens" the "Confidential Case File" to reveal the "suspect's name.

Location:
    Billiard Room

Synopsis:

This appeared to be
a sports-oriented
room. The subject
apparently is
involved in
playing volleyball,
judging from the
equipment taken
into evidence.

VOLLEYBALL

VOLLEYBALL

Kitchen

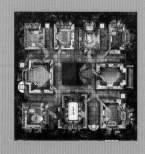

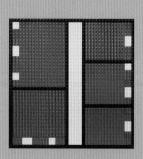

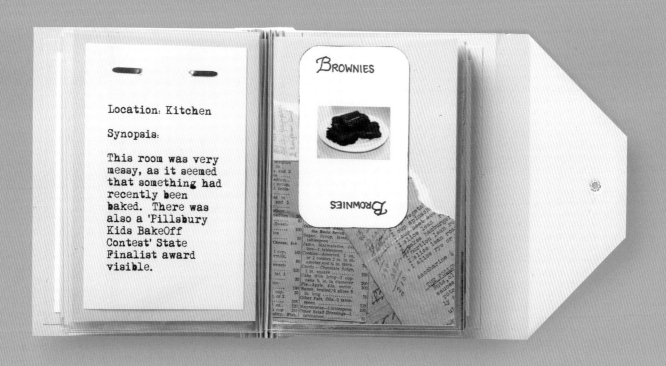

Location: Kitchen

Synopsis:

This room was very messy, as it seemed that something had recently been baked. There was also a 'Pillsbury Kids BakeOff Contest' State Finalist award visible.

BROWNIES

BROWNIES

CHANDRA

CHANDRA

Full Name:
Chandra Kaye Robb

Known Alias:
"Shandy"

CONFIDENTIAL
Case Number: 00045

Date: 8/31/2004

The suspect was brought into custody this evening, and a positive identification given. The minor in question was apprehended at 2130 hours playing 'night games' with her friends. She was cited for curfew violation.

Lori's Approach

← Lori used Chandra's love of the game Clue as a framework for her daughter's tribute album. She discovered that there were patterned papers and embellishments available in a huge variety of special-interest themes, including a complete set for Clue. Check your scrapbook supply store for patterned papers that feature the classic games and toys you and your family love like Scrabble, Clue, Monopoly, Life, Lego, Candyland and others.

"'Once Upon a Quilt' tells the story of each quilt in my family's collection, including who made the quilt, if it was made especially for some-one, the date it was made and the story behind the quilt."

Who accidentally washed one of Lisa's prized quilts in bleach and turned the back of the quilt white?

Find out about this mishap and many other stories in Lisa Foust Moorefield's tribute album about her family and the family quilt collection. The quilts Lisa describes are not made merely to protect against the cold; they are expressions of family love, and painstaking artistry. Scrapbooking them is a wonderful way to pay tribute to, and document, loving family relationships, family history and Lisa's own hopes and dreams.

BUNNIES
Made by Lisa Foust (Moorefield)
1990

This was my first quilt. I saw the pattern for this baby quilt in the fabric store where I worked, and thought it was really cute. It stayed folded in my hope chest for eleven years until Scarlett was born.

LISA MOOREFIELD

I taught myself how to quilt in 1990 when I made my first quilt. My true interest and passion for quilting developed eleven years later when I made several more quilts. My favorite aspects of quilting are fabric selection and hand-quilting. I like to admire the quilts I've made, but my true joy comes from watching my children play and sleep with them.

Through Lisa's "Once Upon a Quilt" album we learn about a grandmother's quilting style and personality, and about the quilt she lovingly made for a college-bound grandson. Lisa also tells us the story of her own love of quilting and how she looked forward to having her own family. We know from Lisa's journaling, for example, that daughter Scarlett's quilt was made eleven years before she was born! We know too that once her own family expanded, Lisa's lovingly-made quilts followed in rapid succession.

Any aspect of family life or history can be a way to document details that are otherwise not recorded. Where else in Lisa's life would there be a place to record that husband Rickey accidentally washed one of the quilts in bleach and turned a pale blue backing white, or that he was very apologetic? Themed albums give you a way to preserve these small but telling details of family life.

PATRIOTIC
Made by Lisa Moorefield
Especially for Holden Moorefield (son)
August 2003

Scarlett protested when I tried to use "her" baby quilts, so I made one just for Holden. Since he was born on the 4th of July, the obvious choice was to use patriotic fabric. I worked on it when Holden was taking naps. Scarlett played with fabric squares while I sewed. It is the fastest and easiest quilt I've made.

Made with love by
Mommy

KALEIDOSCOPE
Made by Lisa Moorefield
Especially for Rickey Moorefield (husband)
April 2003

I contemplated making this quilt for two years, and finally decided that it was "now or never" (since I was six months pregnant with Holden). This is a queen-size quilt and the most time-consuming one I've made so far. I used many different fabrics, including scraps from Scarlett's dresses and previous quilts. I cut the fabric pieces using a rotary cutter and mat, a process which took almost as long as sewing the pieces together! This is one of my favorite quilts; I love the kaleidoscope pattern and happy colors. Scarlett and Holden like looking at all the different fabrics on the quilt, and especially like finding the three tractors.

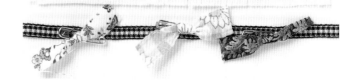

BESSIE MOOREFIELD

Mrs. Moorefield always had a quilting frame hanging from her bedroom ceiling during the winter. Neighbors and relatives would gather there every afternoon to quilt and gossip. Mrs. Moorefield was particular about quilting: if she didn't like the quality of someone's quilting, she would remove the stitches and re-quilt it after everyone left. Mrs. Moorefield made numerous quilts, and most of them were quilted in her trademark "fan" pattern.

RED
Made by Bessie Moorefield
Especially for Rickey Moorefield (grandson)
1972

Mrs. Moorefield made this twin-size quilt for Rickey just before he left for college, and she made it six inches longer to accommodate the longer beds in college dorms. I replaced the binding in 2001 because it had become frayed and torn.

Lisa's Approach

In keeping with the theme of her album, Lisa's album cover is a 14 x 14 quilt with many small beads and a woven label sewn on. Her journaling is textile-themed too. It's printed on white fabric that has been taped to cardstock and run through an inkjet printer. The fabric journaling is then sewed to white cardstock. The edges have been frayed to highlight the fabric feel. The small, square photos in the bottom corners of her layouts are close-ups of the quilt backs, as well as embellishments that provide more visual interest to the page.

Blessed are the
children of quilters,
for they shall
inherit the quilts.

MYSTERY QUILTS

Rickey inherited two flying geese quilts and a hexagon quilt from his aunt Billie Alexander. He thinks they were made by his grandmother, Bessie Moorefield.

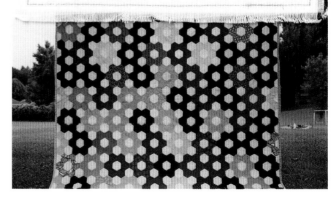

There are many different ways to scrapbook a tribute album. Each is as unique as the family, family member, friend, pet, place or organization that the album honors. Resist the temptation to try to scrapbook everything about your subject. It's too time consuming and may very well dissuade you from undertaking the project. Focusing on a smaller range of time or activity allows you to tell the story more clearly and with more feeling.

Framing a Tribute Album

The albums featured in this chapter of **Scrapbooks to Cherish** pay tribute to families using the unique frames of home, quilts, heritage language and a board game. Other frame ideas for tribute albums include:

The man/woman/mom/dad/brother/son who can fix anything

Talents/hobbies/games/sports/awards/accomplishments

Our family recipes and the stories behind them

Things I love most about you

The clothes you wore

A week in the life of . . .

Sights, sounds and tastes of your hometown

How our home/family grew

How does your garden grow?

Our family's military service

Family holiday traditions

Stories from your childhood

Tributes from your friends and family

You say the funniest things

The A—Z of you

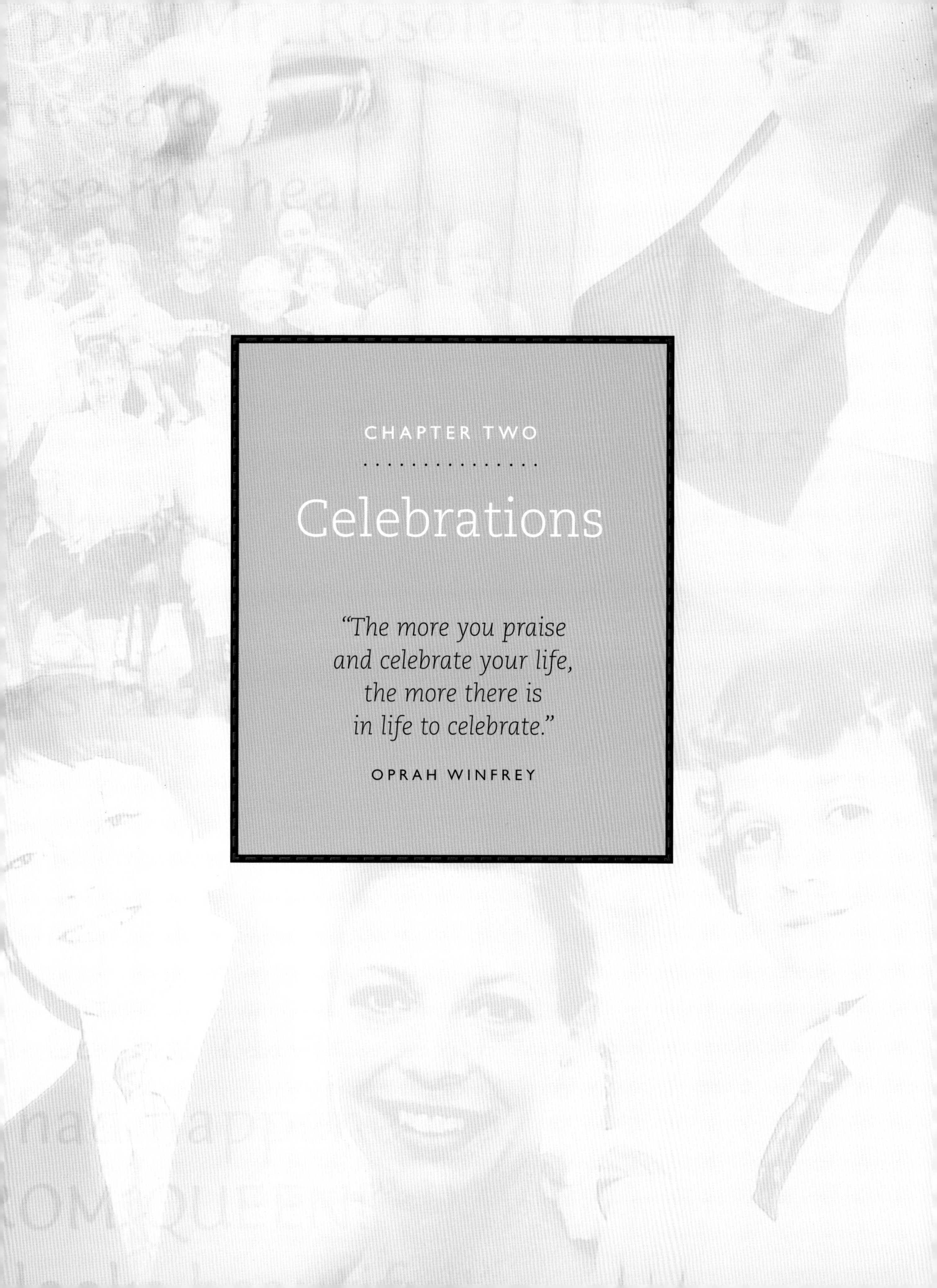

CHAPTER TWO

Celebrations

*"The more you praise
and celebrate your life,
the more there is
in life to celebrate."*

OPRAH WINFREY

Millions of photos are taken every year and the vast majority of them are snapped at celebrations. These include birthdays, retirements, school events, the arrival of new babies, reunions, weddings and the many, many more events that supportive family and friends share.

A look at our winning celebrations albums shows how family members or friends can make such functions live on forever through a lovingly made scrapbook. We bet **Nancy Kreider's**  daughter Katey will enjoy her relationship album forever. Read about mother and daughter as the two help transform Katey from a pony-tailed sports jock to a princess ready for prom. Then see what happens, and how Nancy documents what the big evening brings.

Glitter and glamour are not the subjects of **Nancy Nally's** family reunion album, but there is a lot of  family—and a lot of love. Nancy scrapbooked this album with so much feeling that we wanted to be at the family reunion with her. We could feel the love and support of her extended family coming right off the pages.

And what could be more of a celebration than a wedding? See how **Dot Keil's** guest album for her sister  and new brother-in-law, Robin and Ken, was used as one of the most joyful parts of the wedding day itself, and how it continues to be a treasure of memories for the new family, even today.

We hope you'll enjoy these celebration albums and the suggestions we have for you to scrapbook some of your own festivities. Get that camera ready. You're going to need it.

Dear Katey,

Your prom will be something I will remember always. The shopping trip to King of Prussia is something I truly enjoyed, not only because we came home with the "perfect dress," but because we spent time together doing "girl stuff"—shopping and gossiping! I'll never forget how long you waited for a dressing room, watching that one girl come out each time in a dress that looked terrible on her! And eating lunch (me) and you starting to cry because you thought you would never find a dress! I'll always remember seeing you in the dressing room at Bloomingdale's with this gorgeous dress and sweat socks sticking out! Even then it looked beautiful on you! We both kept saying, "I can't believe we got the dress!" I guess we both expected to be spending more time at the mall (darn!)

The day of the prom I was nervous and excited for you. I couldn't wait to see you all dressed up. I have to say when I saw your hair done while you were still dressed in jeans and a denim shirt; I wasn't so sure I liked it. BUT after I saw you in your dress, makeup, jewelry, and shoes, you honestly took my breath away. You were absolutely gorgeous! I remember standing in your bedroom singing, "I feel pretty!" Thanks for putting up with me even though you wanted to go to sleep! I'll always treasure that time we spent until 4:10 a.m.—talking! You have always been a beautiful person on the inside. That night your beauty shone through on the outside as well. It's like Mr. Rosolie said—you stole the show! I hope you had a wonderful time and made memories to carry with you always. I love you.
MOM"

When she got home at 4:10 in the morning, Katey Kreider had something really special to tell her mom.

"Prom: A Night to Remember" truly belongs in the Celebrations category. Not only is it a remembrance of a traditional high school celebration—the Prom—it is also a celebration of special mother and daughter moments.

In her album, Nancy captures the fun of watching her daughter

The Dress

Mom and I went shopping for my prom dress at the end of March at King of Prussia Mall. We were ready to spend as "long as it takes" to find *the* dress! (That was a warning for Dad and Mike not to expect us for dinner!) I had an idea of what I wanted-a one-shouldered, straight dress, possibly with a slit up the side, in a bright color. After going into the first four department stores and not seeing anything close (and not trying anything on), Mom was getting frustrated and I was getting worried. Mom knew we were at a stalemate, so ...what else could we do but go eat! After lunch and a pep talk we went into two more department stores and then into the Jessica McClintock store, which was crowded! After waiting 25 minutes for a dressing room I tried on three dresses. I found a dress I liked but it was one size too big.The store would not hold the dress while we looked elsewhere but we took our chances anyway. we went to Bloomingdale's and found the same dress in my size! As soon as I tried it on, we both knew-that was *THE* dress! Better yet, it was $5 cheaper at Bloomie's. Mission accomplished!

transform from a "jock," usually found in gym shorts and a ponytail, into a stylish young woman whose family and friends are ecstatic when she is crowned prom queen.

The album serves as a way to relive the mother-and-daughter shopping and preparations for the special event, and the event itself. The night this album celebrates will never be forgotten, not only because it was so special, but also because Nancy took time to tell the story.

To the Prom in style!

Shoes & Accessories

The next step was the shoes. I thought I might have trouble finding shoes in my size, but we were on a mission and we ended up finding them at the Bon-Ton in Park City. Rather than try and match the color of the dress we decided to go with silver shoes and accessories, which turned out to be a good decision! We found the earrings and bracelet in Boscov's, as well as the purse. Next, I signed up for some tanning sessions in Willow Street. Melissa Kile and I signed up together. The night before the prom I went to Kendig Square to get my nails done for the first time! It took a whole lot longer than I thought-it almost made Dad and I late for the 76er's playoff game! The day of the prom I went to Brenda Feeney's to get my hair and make-up done. Melissa Kile was there helping. It took a LOT of bobby pins and a LOT of hair spray! I even had a headache form the bobby pins poking me in the scalp! But the result was worth it!

Nancy's Approach

Nancy purposely kept the cover of Katey's album blank because the color matched the prom purse and shoes so perfectly. The papers were all chosen because they too reflected the silver and fuchsia of Katey's dress and accessories.

Everyone met at Brian Henry's for pictures with the limo. The whole gang: Jonathan Stevens, Sarah Weaver, Brian Henry, Mike Lowry, Kelly McClune, Brian Miller, Katey, Richie McClune, Megan Ellis.

The phone rang around 10:00 p.m.. Mr. Rosolie, the high school principal was on the phone. He said, "You're not going to believe what just happened." Of course my heart dropped into my stomach and thought it was something bad. "What happened?" He said, "You're daughter was just named Prom Queen!" I shouted "WHAT? Katey?" Michael came running from upstairs and Dad thought something bad had happened until I yelled, "KATEY WAS JUST CROWNED PROM QUEEN!" Mr. Rosolie congratulated me and said, "She looks beautiful!" Karen Baughman, Katey's kindergarten teacher grabbed the phone and was laughing and congratulating me. She said, "She looks gorgeous! I voted for her!" I was so excited for you. This was definitely a "Night to Remember"! We were thrilled for you!

Roses are red,
Violets are blue,
Softball All-star,
Now PROM QUEEN, too!

This was the note I wrote and taped to the TV in the basement so you could see it when you all came back after the post prom party. Of course, everyone was too tired, so they all went home. What a weekend-76er's playoff game, Prom, and Softball All-Star banquet! Whew!

Brian called us from the limo on your way to the post prom party. "Guess what your daughter did?" "I don't know, what did she do?" (trying to act surprised). "She became Prom Queen!" "NO!" "YES!" "How does it feel to go to the prom with the Prom Queen?" "AWESOME!" Next we talked with Katey. "HEY! Way to go!" "Thanks!" "Were you surprised?" "Yea!" "Do you have a tiara?" "Yes!" "Are you still wearing it?" "YES!" "Well, enjoy it! You looked gorgeous tonight!!"

Post Prom Party

After the prom ended it was off to the post prom party at Solanco HS. This year's theme was "A Night At The Oscar's". The Great Hall was decorated beautifully! There was a red carpet for the couples to walk down, complete with paparazzi! Each side of the red carpet had floor tiles with painted hand prints of the seniors, which they did during their lunch period. There was karaoke, video games, videos, basketball, volleyball, ping-pong and more. Katey even had a caricature of herself drawn! The cafeteria had blackjack tables and its own "Planet Hollywood" cafe-complete with hamburgers, hot dogs and more. There was a raffle drawing for prizes at the end. Both Katey and Brian each won $50. Do I sense a shopping trip coming on soon? It was a great ending to a fun and exciting night.

Brent Landis & Katey
Prom King & Prom Queen
2003

"We all relaxed and just enjoyed being together."

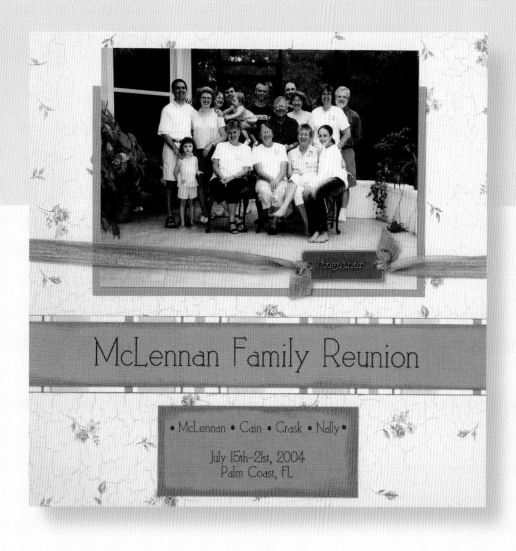

Did the heirloom dresser that Uncle George made in high school make its long-distance journey to the McLennan family reunion safely?

The "McLennan Family Reunion" album was made to record and celebrate the family being together for the first time in a few years, and after several family tragedies. Nancy wanted to capture the feelings of love and togetherness that were shared during the reunion. The album is a delightful glimpse of relatives, young and old, along with touching tributes and little snippets of McLennan family history like Uncle George's dresser.

In Loving Memory

Mom & Poppy McLennan

Nancy's Approach

The photos for Nancy's "McLennan Family Reunion" album were of many different faces and places. This presented a design challenge for her. Converting the photos to black-and-white was not a good solution for this project because the rich colors of Florida's sand, sea and palm trees said so much about the where and when of the reunion. Nancy ultimately presented her family reunion photos in a unified way by using a distinct and consistent color scheme of cream, green and purple.

Allan Cain

These pages are dedicated in loving memory of those who are gone but not forgotten.

Although you may be absent from this earth, you are forever in our hearts.

MCLENNAN FAMILY REUNION SOUTHERN BUS TOUR
JULY 2004 - PALM COAST, FL

Mike designed this logo, complete with the "peach" in the back window of the bus, for the t-shirts that everyone wore on Saturday. The shirts were a huge hit with everyone!

Sure, it's a PEACH...

Mike and Bridget modeling Mike's design on the t-shirts.

Journaling: Since they were driving to Florida, John & Melanie surprised Joan by bringing her the dresser she wanted from her parents' home. It was built by her Uncle George when he was in high school, and it had been in first her grandmother's and then her mother's home as long as she could remember.

→

McLennan Heirloom

Since they were driving to Florida, John & Melanie surprised Joan by bringing her the dresser she wanted from her parents' home. It was built by her Uncle George when he was in high school and had been in first her grandmother's and then her mother's home as long as she could remember.

Second Cousins are

First Class

family

Bridget really loved playing with her second cousins Adam and Sara, and they couldn't get enough of her either! They were wonderful help at keeping her entertained while the grown-ups visited. At our dinner at the club, they all looked so wonderful in their "dress-up" clothes. Sara was especially proud of how Bridget looked in her pretty dress from the Gap, since she had helped pick it out on the girls' shopping trip to the outlet mall!

special

FUN

Till We Gather Again...

May the road rise to meet you

May the wind be always at your back

May the sun shine warm upon your face

The rains fall soft upon your fields.

family

Robin & Ken, Wedding Guest Book

"This album is a gift for my sister and her new husband. I am commemorating the relationship they have together as well as the relationships they have with the guests at their wedding. The overall emotion I want to capture is love."

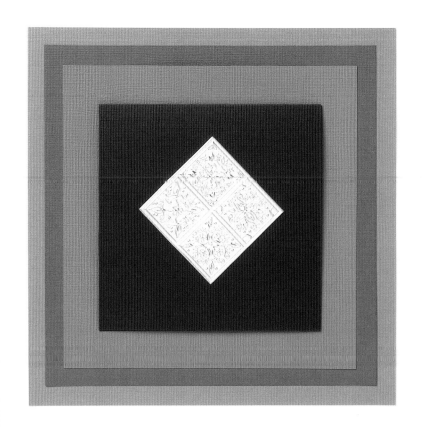

When family and friends attended Robin and Ken's wedding, they were moved to find their own photos in the bride and groom's guest book.

Dot's sister and her then-fiancé asked Dot to make them a scrapbook that could be used as a guest book at their wedding. Dot wanted to use the opportunity to celebrate more than just the wedding couple. She wanted to honor all of the guests and their unique relationships to the couple. So she made the her "Robin & Ken, Wedding Guest Book" interactive. Dot featured each guest in a special section where they could write a personal message to the couple. Previously taken pictures of the guests were mounted on the outside of each section. On the inside of each section, Dot later mounted pictures taken at the wedding. This allowed the album to be a memorable keepsake from the wedding couple's special day. It truly is a celebration of the union of many lives.

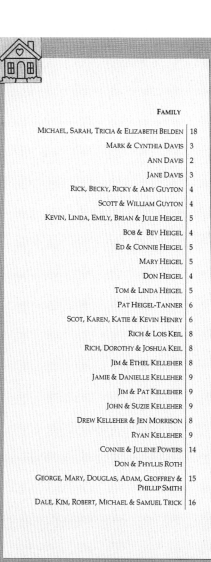

FAMILY

MICHAEL, SARAH, TRICIA & ELIZABETH BELDEN	18
MARK & CYNTHIA DAVIS	3
ANN DAVIS	2
JANE DAVIS	3
RICK, BECKY, RICKY & AMY GUYTON	4
SCOTT & WILLIAM GUYTON	4
KEVIN, LINDA, EMILY, BRIAN & JULIE HEIGEL	5
BOB & BEV HEIGEL	4
ED & CONNIE HEIGEL	5
MARY HEIGEL	5
DON HEIGEL	4
TOM & LINDA HEIGEL	5
PAT HEIGEL-TANNER	6
SCOT, KAREN, KATIE & KEVIN HENRY	6
RICH & LOIS KEIL	8
RICH, DOROTHY & JOSHUA KEIL	8
JIM & ETHEL KELLEHER	8
JAMIE & DANIELLE KELLEHER	9
JIM & PAT KELLEHER	9
JOHN & SUZIE KELLEHER	9
DREW KELLEHER & JEN MORRISON	8
RYAN KELLEHER	9
CONNIE & JULENE POWERS	14
DON & PHYLLIS ROTH	
GEORGE, MARY, DOUGLAS, ADAM, GEOFFREY & PHILLIP SMITH	15
DALE, KIM, ROBERT, MICHAEL & SAMUEL TRICK	16

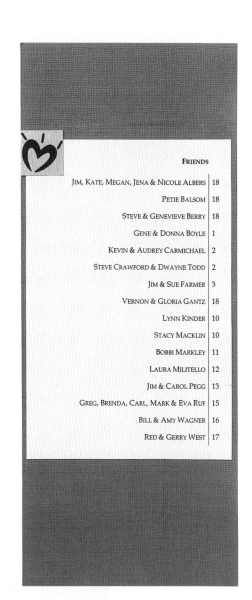

FRIENDS

JIM, KATE, MEGAN, JENA & NICOLE ALBERS	18
PETIE BALSOM	18
STEVE & GENEVIEVE BERRY	18
GENE & DONNA BOYLE	1
KEVIN & AUDREY CARMICHAEL	2
STEVE CRAWFORD & DWAYNE TODD	2
JIM & SUE FARMER	3
VERNON & GLORIA GANTZ	18
LYNN KINDER	10
STACY MACKLIN	10
BOBBI MARKLEY	11
LAURA MILITELLO	12
JIM & CAROL PEGG	13
GREG, BRENDA, CARL, MARK & EVA RUF	15
BILL & AMY WAGNER	16
RED & GERRY WEST	17

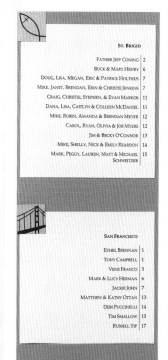

ST. BRIGID

FATHER JEFF CONING	2
BUCK & MARY HENRY	6
DOUG, LISA, MEGAN, ERIC & PATRICK HOLTHUS	7
MIKE, JANET, BRENDAN, ERIN & CHRISTIE JENKINS	7
CRAIG, CHRISTIE, STEPHEN, & EVAN MARKOS	11
DANA, LISA, CAITLYN & COLLEEN McDANIEL	11
MIKE, ROBIN, AMANDA & BRENDAN MEYER	12
CAROL, RYAN, OLIVIA & JOE MYERS	12
JIM & BECKY O'CONNOR	13
MIKE, SHELLY, NICK & EMILY REARDON	14
MARK, PEGGY, LAUREN, MATT & MICHAEL SCHWEITZER	15

SAN FRANCISCO

ETHEL BRENNAN	1
TONY CAMPBELL	1
VENE FRANCO	3
MARK & LUCY HERMAN	6
JACKIE JOHN	7
MATTHEW & KATHY OTTAN	13
DEBI PUCCINELLI	14
TIM SMALLOW	15
RUSSELL YIP	17

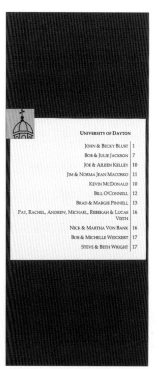

UNIVERSITY OF DAYTON

JOHN & BECKY BLUST	1
BOB & JULIE JACKSON	7
JOE & AILEEN KELLEY	10
JIM & NORMA JEAN MACOSKO	11
KEVIN McDONALD	10
BILL O'CONNELL	12
BRAD & MARGIE PINNELL	13
PAT, RACHEL, ANDREW, MICHAEL, REBEKAH & LUCAS VIETH	16
NICK & MARTHA VON BANK	16
BOB & MICHELLE WEICKERT	17
STEVE & BETH WRIGHT	17

WISH YOU WERE HERE

Dot's Approach

In the guest book Dot made, she scrapbooked a picture and a journaling block, for each guest family, arranged alphabetically by last name. She also used icons to indicate how the wedding couple is related to the guest (church friends, college friends, family, and friends from San Francisco). Dot printed the icons on metallic paper and used them like stickers.

Dot scanned and printed the outside photos in black and white for a consistent look. Many of these photos were taken at pre-wedding events such as the engagement party and the bridal showers. The bride and groom supplied most of the others. Dot mounted the photos on a 5 x 5 flap (5 x 10 page folded in half). She then

15

mounted them, four to a page, using a consistent color scheme. The icons representing the type of relationship each guest had to the couple were mounted on the inner corner of each picture. Inside each flap Dot adhered a 4 x 4 insert, labeled with the guests' names. This insert was provided for the guests to journal messages to the couple. The top portion of the flap holds a picture of each guest taken at the wedding.

Robin & Ken,
THANK YOU FOR SHARING YOUR
SPECIAL DAY WITH ME.
MANY YEARS OF HAPPINESS
& MEMORIES
LOVE,
TIM

TIM SMALLOW

Ken & Robin,
Congratulations!
Thank you for letting
us be part of your special
day! God bless!
Love, George, Doug,
Mary, Scott & Phillip
Adam,

GEORGE, MARY, DOUGLAS, ADAM,
GEOFFREY & PHILLIP SMITH

THE HEIGEL FAMILY

ROBIN & KEN
BEN, MOLLY & SARAH

Often the scrapbooker or photographer at family celebrations is also the one preparing the food and putting up the decorations. To make your busy celebration day run more smoothly, here's a checklist that will make later scrapbooking easier.

Before the Celebration

- Save or photograph a copy of the invitation and the guest list.
- Photograph or note information about preparations. Who helped and how?
- Prepare a folder containing protective sheets to use to gather gift cards, wrapping-paper samples and small decorations.
- If you would like guests to do the journaling for you, prepare cardstock for each guest to write a celebration message.

During the Celebration

- If there are decorations at your celebration, photograph or save a few.
- Make sure every attendee appears in at least one photo. (Others can sometimes be talked into being the photographer if they have a list of what you want photographed.)
- If you have prepared cards for attendees, ask them to write on their card.
- Ask someone to take YOUR photo during the celebration.
- Photograph the outside of the building or location of the celebration.
- If there are games or activities involved, take photos of those too.

After the Celebration

- Use photos of decorations or small, saved decorations as a theme or embellishment for your album pages. Note whether decorations were traditional or based on a hobby, interest or popular cartoon character.
- As you journal, think about the food. If food was involved, was it food traditionally associated with this celebration? Who prepared it?
- Write a few lines describing each person who attended the celebration.

For additional ideas, see *A Simple Guide to Scrapbooking Celebrations*.
Above all, enjoy your celebration and make good memories.

TOTONTEAC

CALIFORNIA

MAR DEL

CHAPTER THREE

. . . .

Self Discovery

*"Who looks outside,
dreams;
who looks inside,
awakens."*

CARL JUNG

Self discovery is by definition a personal journey, but it's often told best when we write it to share with others. **Mou Saha's** album was written for her not-quite-two-year-old daughter at a time when Mou believed she  herself might be dying. The album is full of exotic color combinations and a life lived mainly in India. We think you will be as touched and intrigued by Mou's story as we were.

Jennifer Adams Donnelly wrote and  scrapbooked her self-discovery album as a thirtieth birthday gift to herself. Bound in three small volumes, one for her past, one for her life now, and one for her future dreams, Jennifer's book is a gift to us all. We're sure you'll agree.

The last in our winning self-discovery albums is one that we wish you could touch and see as we were able to.

 **Marnie Flores'** album has so many hidden and unexpected fold outs and envelopes, and each contains powerful stories of this brilliant young woman's life. Her determination shines through the disappointment of not getting into Harvard because a counselor didn't turn in the right paperwork. Her courage continues on in spite of a devastating stroke. But above all, her gratitude for the life and family she now enjoys rings out from her beautifully made album.

Read on to see all our winning self-discovery albums, and to read tips and tricks you can use to get started on a self-discovery album of your own.

"This is an album about me. It is a summary of my life so far. I made it for my daughter so she can learn about me, in case of my death."

With crisp, detective-novel words, Mou Saha begins an album that has brought tears to the eyes of every editor who has read it.

The album "I" is a powerful exploration of Mou's life, made at a time—she was just twenty-nine—when she was threatened by cancer. Mou had made several scrapbook albums, but had never taken the time to focus on her own life. Then she was threatened by cancer. Her only child was a young daughter, barely two years old, and Mou feared the little girl might grow up without ever knowing her mother. For Mou, this was as alarming as the possibility of having cancer. In the six days between her mammography and the subsequent biopsy, Mou focused on making a legacy scrapbook for her daughter.

Mou chose Toby Keith's song "I Wanna Talk About Me" for her title page. It summed up her feelings of always focusing on others and helped her concentrate on evaluating the meaning in her own life, which she describes as part pleasure cruise and part odyssey.

Mou's goal was to personally convey the essence of who she was to her daughter—and to do it in six days. The deadline pressure of the process was helpful. In those six dedicated days, Mou rediscovered herself, reevaluated her life, took a hard look inside and found a bounty of blessings to count, despite her situation. This gift to her daughter led to a renewed sense of self discovery, and to her "Coolest Album Ever."

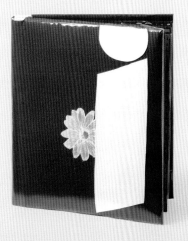

TO YOU
FOR YOU

Dear Nini,
I worked at several scrapbooks and always thought that someday, I'll dedicate one to myself...
hurry to start till...
ay, you may wonder.
ths into nursing, I
in my left breast that
even after nursing.
nosis was a clogged
t a year later, the
led to mammography.
ted abnormal
ctor visits stated a
hich needs immediate
ion and biopsy. The
led for next Friday,
nd I have a week

taking care of as much
aring for the worst, I
night putting things

months old. I am
rrow. But if I
w me!
ng able to
u to
om

From me

Dear Nini,
    I worked at several scrapbooks and always thought that someday, I'll dedicate one to myself...
    I was in no hurry to start till... TODAY. Why today, you may wonder.
    Well, 8 months into nursing, I could feel a lump in my left breast that did not disappear even after nursing. The primary diagnosis was a clogged milk duct. Almost a year later, the annual checkup led to mammography. The results indicated abnormal findings. More doctor visits stated a Fiber Adenoma which needs immediate surgical intervention and biopsy. The surgery is scheduled for next Friday, June 25, 2004. And I have a week before that.
    Apart from taking care of as much as I can and preparing for the worst, I spent one sleepless night putting things in perspective.
    You are only 19 months old. I am 29 and blurry about tomorrow. But if I died today, how will you know me! Apart from my fear of not being able to see you grow up, I really want you to remember me as I truly am...not from the anecdotes of other people who'll dissect me according to their choice.
    None of us really know FUTURE, but I cherish my past and enjoy TODAY. This is my photo journal...all about me. Well, most certainly I'll enjoy the attention. I'm not sure whether we'll read this journal together someday or you'll do so alone, but either way, this will be our connection, me or no me. So Girlfriend, enjoy.

           Love always,
           Mommy.
           6/18/2004.

→

Journaling: Up till 8th grade, I spent more time in extra-curricular activities than in school work. My parents believed that studying books alone is not enough, sports and arts build a person.

Since, I took great interest in swimming and painting, they too encouraged me. As I represented my school in both fields, I was excused for missing classes during inter-school, district and state meets.

I was always moderately good at studies, but never felt the urge to push myself further till I took up a Psychology major. And my grades jumped from B or B+ to A+.

Whatever I did, be it swimming, gymnastics, yoga, badminton, music, painting or school work, I learned that there's no alternative for hard work and loving what you do.

My schooling from kindergarten through high school (1979-1994) was at South Point High School, Calcutta, India. It was Asia's largest school and a premiere educational institution. Not only getting admission but also surviving their high standards was difficult for many. That's why every year at least five students ranked highest in the public exams.

By the time I was in 8th grade, I had decided to become a Counselor and a professor of Psychology. From then on, I took steps

education

My schooling from kindergarten through high school (1979-1994) was at South Point High School, Calcutta, India. It was Asia's largest school and a premiere educational institution. Not only getting admission but also surviving their high standards was difficult for many. That's why every year at least five students ranked highest in the public exams.

By the time I was in 8th grade, I had decided to become a Counselor and a professor of Psychology. From then on, I took steps accordingly. In my higher secondary courses, I opted for Psychology and loved it so much that later on I took it up as major in my Bachelor's course. This is when I really took interest in school work and it paid off big time too. I loved doing Psychometry much to my own surprise, because I wasn't too fond of math, other than algebra. My ability to strike up a conversation with most people helped me greatly in establishing rapport with clients. I didn't mind spending all day at the library reading far beyond course work. India, particularly, Calcutta is not known for much work in Psychology, so I started thinking about schools in other states, which however, was a difficult search because I had no access to internet. But I met a wonderful teacher, Prof. Prabhat K. Mukherjee whose teachings helped me with life in general. However, this is also the stage of life where I learned another unpleasant truth...how petty politics plagues an institution, even an educational one. I graduated in 1999, topping in Calcutta University, with marks unheard of in the Department's history.

After I came to USA, I wanted to continue with my Ph.D. But now I had to accommodate Ashis's schedules. We couldn't move from Florida. I couldn't go to a school of my choice, couldn't afford the expenses, couldn't apply for a scholarship or get a job as I didn't have green card or student visa, didn't have the time to study or Ashis's support. All I had was my indomitable desire to go to an American school. Finally, I did go to University of South Florida and completed a course in Marriage and Family Therapy with a GPA of 4 and I enjoyed learning about American way of schooling more than anything else.

extra-curricular

Up till 8th grade, I spent more time in extra-curricular activities than in school work. My parents believed that studying books alone is not enough, sports and arts build a person.

Since, I took great interest in swimming and painting, they too encouraged me. As I represented my school in both fields, I was excused for missing classes during inter-school, district and state meets.

I was always moderately good at studies, but never felt the urge to push myself further till I took up Psychology major. And my grades jumped from B or B+ to A+.

Whatever I did, be it swimming, gymnastics, yoga, badminton, music, painting or school work, I learned that there's no alternative for hard work and loving what you do.

1982

accordingly. In my higher secondary courses, I opted for Psychology and loved it so much that later on I took it up as a major in my Bachelor's course. This is when I really took interest in school work and it paid off big time too. I loved doing Psychometry much to my own surprise, because I wasn't too fond of math, other than algebra. My ability to strike up a conversation with most people helped me greatly in establishing rapport with clients. I didn't mind spending all day at the library reading far beyond course work.

India, particularly Calcutta is not known for much work in Psychology, so I started thinking about schools in other states, which however was a difficult search because I had no access to Internet. But I met a wonderful teacher, Prof. Prabhat K. Mukherjee, whose teachings helped me with life in general. However, this is also the stage of life where I learned another unpleasant truth...how petty politics plagues an institution, even an educational one. I graduated in 1999, topping in Calcutta University, with marks unheard of in the Department's history.

After I came to the USA, I wanted to continue with my Ph. D. but now I had to accommodate Ashis's schedules. We couldn't move from Florida. I couldn't go to a school of my choice, couldn't apply for a scholarship or get a job as I didn't have a green card or student visa, didn't have the time to study or Ashis's support. All I had was my indomitable desire to go to an American school. Finally, I did go the University of South Florida and completed a course in Marriage and Family Therapy with a GPA of 4 and I enjoyed learning about American way of schooling more than anything else.

Young and in love

I was about 14 when I first fell in love...the boy who stole my heart was in 9th grade while I was in the 8th. He was tall and very very handsome. In a crowd, he'll be the one to catch your eyes...well, many other girls had crushes on him. Like real cool guys, he acted unaware of his charm, and sadly for me, he was unaware of me too till he joined another school.

Meanwhile, I was so enchanted by him that I never paid attention to the boys who vied for my awareness. May be at 15, I was more in love with love itself and fancy of having a boyfriend was more charming than having a real relationship.

Then, I started 9th grade. Two guys became my friends the very first day. At that time, it was beyond my wildest imagination, that one of them was to be my boyfriend one day.

Four years later, both of us realized that we had deeper feelings for each than just friendship. We sought each other in trouble, in pain, in loneliness...the relation lasted for a few months, before we understood that we were not destined to be together... after a lot of heartache, I came to terms with myself and moved on with the lessons learned from the experience. But I never entered another relationship till I got married.

Our wedding was arranged by our parents. We were strangers to each other. Ain't life funny? The person you know most becomes a stranger and an unknown becomes your soul mate!

Journaling: I was about 14 when I first fell in love. . . the boy who stole my heart was in 9th grade while I was in the 8th. He was tall and very very handsome. In a crowd, he'll be the one to catch your eyes. . . well, many other girls had crushes on him. Like real cool guys, he acted unaware of his charm, and sadly for me, he was unaware of me too till he joined another school.

Meanwhile, I was so enchanted by him that I never paid attention to the boys who vied for my awareness. Maybe at 15 I was more in love with love itself, and the fancy of having a boyfriend was more charming than having a real relationship.

Then, I started 9th grade. Two guys became my friends the very first day. At that time, it was beyond my wildest imagination that one of them was to be my boyfriend one day.

Four years later, both of us realized that we had deeper feelings for each than just friendship. We sought each other in trouble, in pain, in loneliness. . .the relationship lasted for a few months, before we understood that we were not destined to be together. . .after a lot of heartache, I came to terms with myself and moved on with the lessons learned from the experience. But I never entered another relationship till I got married.

Our wedding was arranged by our parents. We were strangers to each other. Ain't life funny? The person you know most becomes a stranger and an unknown becomes your soul mate!

Journaling: I was born in Calcutta, West Bengal, India at 8:20 am on September 5, 1974 to Atul and Minati Saha, their second child, born after their son died at 2 months of age the previous year. My maternal grandpa passed away while my mom was pregnant with me. I grew up as an only child.

My family did not possess a camera at the time. So either we had to go to a studio or some friends of the family took our pictures. Each photo shoot used to be a big event. This photo of me trying to bathe myself is one of my first.

My aunt chose my name, "MOU." It means 'honey' in our mother tongue, Bengali. It was intended to be my pet name till a more formal one was agreed upon. But somehow everyone thought that the small and sweet name suited me very well, most so my mom who gave up her teaching career for me.

Later, anybody who asked my name would wait for something more to follow after I said it. Such a short first name was not quite common. However, I became more popularly known as 'Honeybee' among my peers after a Bengali nursery rhyme. Probably that shaped my personality too. My motto became, "I do not mess with you if you do not mess with me!" One of my American college professors once told me, "Mou, you remind me of a leopard: peaceful, self-content, yet swift in the face of danger. Very relaxed and agile at the same time." Aha aha, Year of the TIGER, remember!

Much later, I learned that MOU was a unit of land measurement in ancient China and of course, there is the Memorandum of Understanding.

After I came to the USA, people had a real tough time pronouncing my name. . . and I became 'Mew,' 'Moo,' 'Moa,' 'Moe,' 'Mia,' 'Mou,' 'Mow' and finally 'Mo.'

I still remember my FIRST day of school. It was January, 1979. Bursting with anticipation, I could hardly contain my excitement. New books, supplies, meeting new people... I marched right into my class, where many of the kids looked scared. Some were crying. I went to console one of them. Later on, she became my friend.

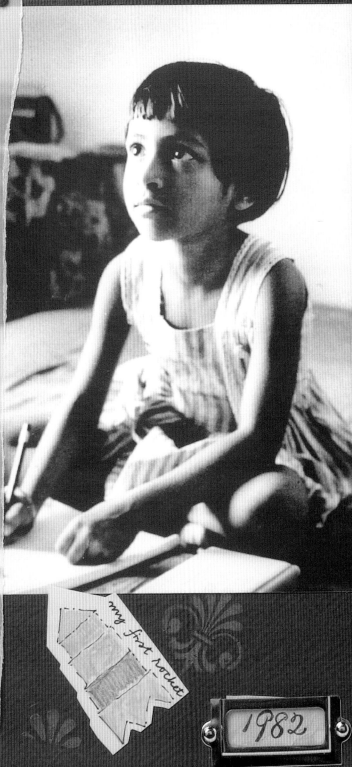

Nin...

...I was 1½ and loved looking at pictures. Despite her day's hard work, mom still made time to cut out pictures from old calendars and magazines and pasted them in our first scrapbook together.

As I grew older, I started making my own scrapbooks which later included photos too. We had no concept of archival ... ut mom still has our brittle, ...-eaten, water-damaged first ... espite all our moves.

IMAGINE!

... year, I was drawing on the fl... chalks. My first meaningful drawing was that of a rocket.

From the time I was 9, I started entering sit-and-draw art contests and won many prizes and awards. After a year, we no longer had to buy art supplies. All that I needed came from prizes and gifts.

At 12, I got published in an acclaimed magazine and two other newspapers. At 13, I won the Government of India Centre for Cultural Resources and Training Scholarship ... inting. I kept winning the same till I was ... ut-off age.

INSPIRE

... people said that I should pursue a ... art. But I didn't have enough faith ... ent. So, I followed the course of ...instream education. I knew that I wanted to be a Counselor and still could enjoy painting and crafts at leisure. So, I became a Counselor.

Then I got married, had you. What used to be my main work became sidetracked. I have no regrets whatsoever.

However, I started realizing that the little time that I can make just for myself is best spent in art. The moment I pick up my paintbrush, I'm transformed to a different world. What I enjoy most is scrapbooking because it allows me to bring together everything I love – crafts, photography, journaling, the art of layout and most importantly my fond experiences...it just keeps me going!

my first rocket

1982

our wedding

WEDDING...well! The highlight was the speed at which things progressed. I'll just include a CALENDAR OF EVENTS.

*June 1998: My parents responded to a matrimonial ad.

*July '98: The Sarkar family came to check us out.

*Oct 3, '98: Ashis came to our house with his brother-in-law. We didn't even talk.

*Oct 4, '98: Both families agreed upon a relationship.

*Oct 7,'98: The Sarkars suddenly decided to match our horoscopes. We were surprised.

*November '98: Ashis's father wrote us a letter saying that our horoscopes were incompatible. The wedding was off. We carried on with our lives.

*April 17,1999: Ashis's dad called asking my mom whether I was married already.

*September 8,'99: Ashis's dad called again. He had kept track of when my M.Sc. exams were over and said if we agreed, the wedding can take place on Nov. 23,'99. We were more surprised this time.

*Sep. 15,'99: I applied for international passport.

*Sep. 18,'99: Ashis called my dad from USA asking his permission to call me. A telephone courtship followed over the next 2 months after he apologized for the ordeal

* Oct. 8,'99: My parents and I went for a vacation to South India much to Ashis's mom's dismay. Ashis called me up in the hotels we stayed in.

*Nov 5,'99: We returned 4 days after our scheduled return due to bad weather .

*Nov 6-21,'99: Shopping for dresses, jewelry and everything else continued.

*Nov 22,'99: My passport arrived.

*Nov 23,'99: THE WEDDING

*Nov 24,'99: I went to Ashis's house in Chinsurah.

*Nov 25,'99: The Bridal Reception

*Nov 28,'99: We came back to visit my parents.

*Nov 29,'99: I applied for and got my visa.

*Nov 30-Dec 8,'99: Back and forth between Calcutta and Chinsurah, shopping, visiting people, other formalities.

*Dec 9,'99: We started out from Chinsurah, met my parents at the airport and said goodbye to one and all as I flew back with Ashis to USA .

*Dec 11,'99: We reached Tampa around 1:30pm after missing the previous night's flight. As I crossed the threshold of Ashis's Oak Ramble apartment, we both embarked on our new life together.

November 23, 1999

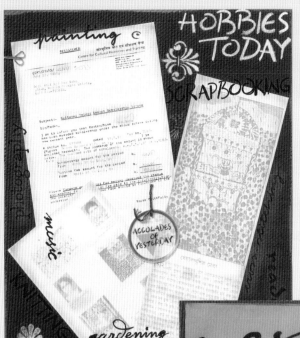

Mou's Approach

 When making her album, Mou turned to the spicy scarlet and saffron colors that reflect the clothing and traditions of her native India. Mou, an accomplished artist, used several tricks to keep the rich colors and the important—if lengthy—journaling from being overwhelming.

All her photos are black and white.

Most of the journaling is done on vellum, which works in quiet harmony with the richly-textured scrapbook pages.

Pockets that hold additional journaling are made of sheer, lace fabric.

Very little patterned paper is used.

Dear Nini,

Enough said so far! This is who I am.

I am scared of changes, yet bored to stick to routines...

I am afraid of many things, specially ghosts and nightmares, yet I sense a strange strength and courage to overcome obstacles.

Patience is not one of my gifts.

I can't lie tactfully.

I am too proud to admit when I'm jealous or hurt.

Sometimes I get sad and then get tired of being sorry for myself and break out of it with fresh energy.

I don't want to go through life wishing I had done this or done that... still, I understand that I won't be able to fulfill all my wishes or those of others. Even though I'm afraid that I might fail, I don't want to regret not trying at all.

And I can go on forever like this.

Look Nini, I don't know whether I have cancer, but I can promise you that as long as I'm around, I won't mope about my life. Life's just too short to be bored.

Another thing, I'm thankful for all that God blessed me with, especially YOU. And I'll love you always, beyond the times when I'm mad at you or when you mess up.

Love always,
Mom
June 24,2004

Never be so serious that you stop enjoying yourself. Learning can happen only with fun.

Failure is scary. The only thing scarier is regretting not trying.

Hold your tongue often. Words can't always be taken back.

If you find it hard to love someone just as they are... before trying to change them, look inwards...if possible, through other's eyes...

In the frame of time, everything is futile. So, even if you mess up 'big time' today, always remember, tomorrow is another day.

I have a feeling that someday when you are a teenager, I might regret some of these advices... but hey! I'll take the chance.

"This book is to celebrate my life, give thanks for what I have, and look forward to the future. It's for me only, as a gift to myself for my 30th birthday. It was a project of true self discovery. I looked back over my life, examined who I am now, and set goals for the future. As a busy mom and wife, I don't always take time to value myself. But I've done an ok job with my life, and I need to appreciate that. I love these books. They give me goose bumps and bring tears to my eyes every time I look through them."

Jennifer appreciates each day as if it were her last. She is a writer and a redhead. She wants to learn to bake bread and teach someone to read.

Jennifer's three small, self-discovery albums are an amazingly rich tapestry of her past—Where I've Been and What I Learned There; her present—Who I Am and Why That's Good; and her goals for the future—What I Want to Do and What That Means. On the small but beautifully crafted pages, she has woven personal history, lessons learned, day-to-day life, personality, relationships and dreams into a tiny treasure that will touch all who read it.

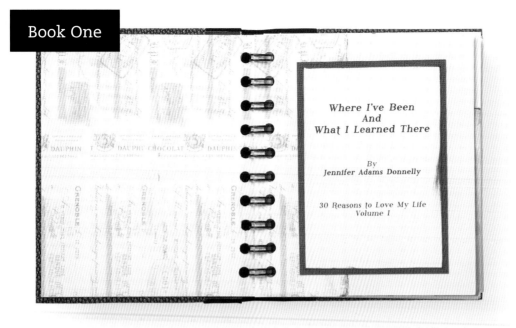

Book One

Where I've Been
And
What I Learned There

By
Jennifer Adams Donnelly

30 Reasons to Love My Life
Volume I

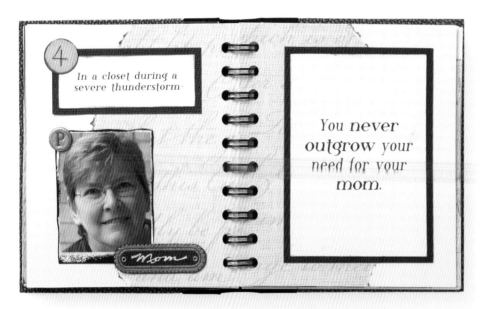

4

In a closet during a
severe thunderstorm

Mom

You never
outgrow your
need for your
mom.

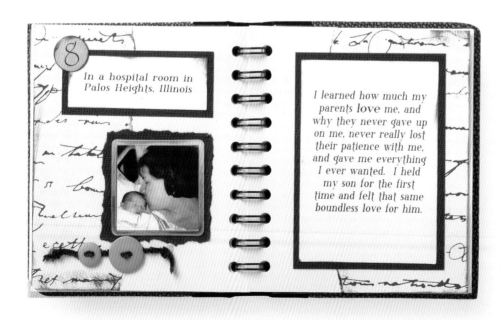

8

In a hospital room in
Palos Heights, Illinois

I learned how much my
parents love me, and
why they never gave up
on me, never really lost
their patience with me,
and gave me everything
I ever wanted. I held
my son for the first
time and felt that same
boundless love for him.

Jennifer's Approach

In March 2004, Jennifer attended Creating Keepsakes University in Nashville, Tennessee and worked on many mini-book projects. She came to realize the value of focusing on a small subject, in order to see more clearly its detail and beauty, and decided to start her self-discovery album.

She began by making a list of 30 things she loved about her life and herself, and she realized that these things could be further divided into three groups of 10, like the three decades of her life. She decided to make the books as "book-like" as possible, even creating a slipcover for her three-volume set.

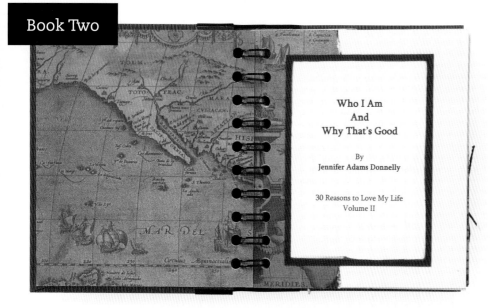

Book Two

Who I Am
And
Why That's Good

By
Jennifer Adams Donnelly

30 Reasons to Love My Life
Volume II

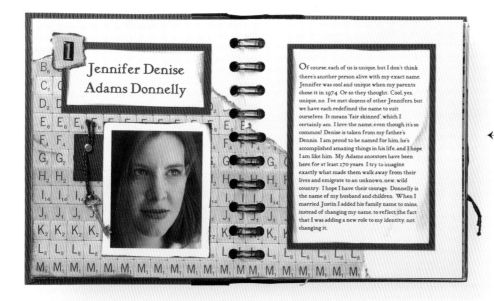

I

Jennifer Denise
Adams Donnelly

Of course, each of us is unique, but I don't think there's another person alive with my exact name. Jennifer was cool and unique when my parents chose it in 1974. Or so they thought. Cool, yes, unique, no. I've met dozens of other Jennifers, but we have each redefined the name to suit ourselves. It means 'fair skinned', which I certainly am. I love the name, even though it's so common! Denise is taken from my father's Dennis. I am proud to be named for him, he's accomplished amazing things in his life, and I hope I am like him. My Adams ancestors have been here for at least 170 years. I try to imagine exactly what made them walk away from their lives and emigrate to an unknown, new, wild country. I hope I have their courage. Donnelly is the name of my husband and children. When I married Justin I added his family name to mine, instead of changing my name, to reflect the fact that I was adding a new role to my identity, not changing it.

Journaling: Of course, each of us is unique, but I don't think there's another person alive with my exact name. Jennifer was cool and unique when my parents chose it in 1974. Or so they thought. Cool yes, unique, no. I've met dozens of other Jennifers, but we have each redefined the name to suit ourselves. It means "fair skinned," which I certainly am. I love the name, even though it's so common. Denise is taken from my father's Dennis. I am proud to be named for him; he's accomplished amazing things in his life, and I hope I am like him. My Adams ancestors have been here for at least 170 years. I try to imagine exactly what made them walk away from their lives and emigrate to an unknown, new, wild country. I hope I have their courage. Donnelly is the name of my husband and children. When I married Justin I added his family name to mine, instead of changing my name, to reflect the the fact that I was adding a new role to my identity, not changing it.

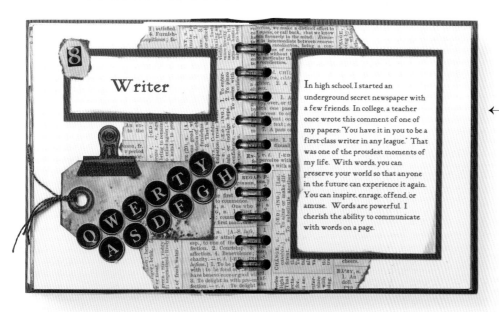

8

Writer

In high school, I started an underground secret newspaper with a few friends. In college, a teacher once wrote this comment of one of my papers: "You have it in you to be a first-class writer in any league." That was one of the proudest moments of my life. With words, you can preserve your world so that anyone in the future can experience it again. You can inspire, enrage, offend, or amuse. Words are powerful. I cherish the ability to communicate with words on a page.

Journaling: In high school I started an underground secret newspaper with a few friends. In college, a teacher once wrote this comment of one of my papers: "You have it in you to be a first-class writer in any league." That was one of the proudest moments of my life. With words, you can preserve your world so that anyone in the the future can experience it again. You can inspire, enrage, offend, or amuse. Words are powerful. I cherish the ability to communicate with words on a page.

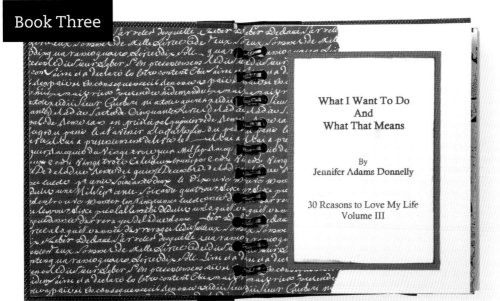

Book Three

What I Want To Do
And
What That Means

By
Jennifer Adams Donnelly

30 Reasons to Love My Life
Volume III

Journaling: Staying organized has always been a struggle. I can easily get everything sorted out and put away, but I have a hard time maintaining order. Finally, I learned that I have a very short attention span, and I get sidetracked on new ideas and projects before I have time to finish and put away the old ones. Books by Marla Cilley ("Flylady") and Julie Morgenstern have helped me to step outside my usual train of thought and set up awesome systems that work for me. The problem with being disorganized is that it's frustrating and expensive, and I really feel angry with myself and don't get much accomplished when my life is mess. I keep working on staying organized, trying to keep all my boats afloat: housework, cooking, kids, friends, hobbies. It's not easy, but the more successful I am, the happier I am, so I will fight clutter for as long as I have to.

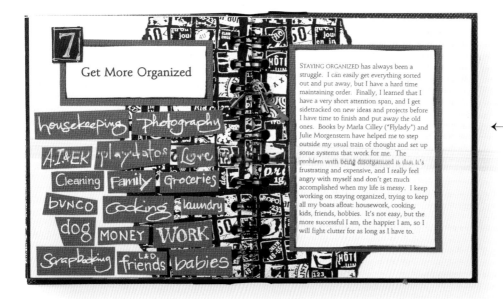

7

Get More Organized

STAYING ORGANIZED has always been a struggle. I can easily get everything sorted out and put away, but I have a hard time maintaining order. Finally, I learned that I have a very short attention span, and I get sidetracked on new ideas and projects before I have time to finish and put away the old ones. Books by Marla Cilley ("Flylady") and Julie Morgenstern have helped me to step outside my usual train of thought and set up some systems that work for me. The problem with being disorganized is that it's frustrating and expensive, and I really feel angry with myself and don't get much accomplished when my life is messy. I keep working on staying organized, trying to keep all my boats afloat: housework, cooking, kids, friends, hobbies. It's not easy, but the more successful I am, the happier I am, so I will fight clutter for as long as I have to.

Journaling: The goal, I think, is purely selfish. I love to cook, and there are few things in life as delicious as fresh, hot bread, with a crisp, golden crust, a slight tang of yeast, sweet and soft and white inside, laced with delicate bubbles of moist air. Spread with a little sweet creamy butter, served alongside a rich bowl of stew. Baking bread is hard work, taking hours, and going beyond the science of a recipe and into the realm of instinct. No recipe can tell you just how to bake, you just have to keep trying until you get it right. I've baked a few loaves, but been disappointed so far. Kneading properly is an art, a lost art, as I know no one who can teach me. But every so often I pull out my jar of yeast and a big bag of flour and start playing. Someday, I will pull from the oven one perfect, crusty, hot loaf of blissful bread, and I will have relearned something precious, something lost for several generations, a treasure regained, never to be lost again.

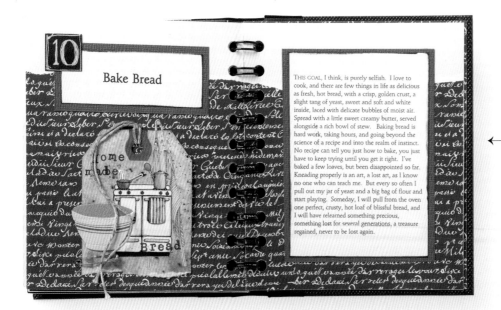

10

Bake Bread

THIS GOAL, I think, is purely selfish. I love to cook, and there are few things in life as delicious as fresh, hot bread, with a crisp, golden crust, a slight tang of yeast, sweet and soft and white inside, laced with delicate bubbles of moist air. Spread with a little sweet creamy butter, served alongside a rich bowl of stew. Baking bread is hard work, taking hours, and going beyond the science of a recipe and into the realm of instinct. No recipe can tell you how to bake, you just have to keep trying until you get it right. I've baked a few loaves, but been disappointed so far. Kneading properly is an art, a lost art, as I know no one who can teach me. But every so often I pull out my jar of yeast and a big bag of flour and start playing. Someday, I will pull from the oven one perfect, crusty, hot loaf of blissful bread, and I will have relearned something precious, something lost for several generations, a treasure regained, never to be lost again.

"I was hoping to leave behind a book my children can read to better understand me as a person and not just as their mother. It was also a chance to think about my life and to express my gratitude for the wonderful journey that I've had thus far."

Marnie Flores became starkly aware of life's fragility when, before turning thirty, she suffered a life-altering stroke.

Marnie's self-discovery album "My First 35 Miles" is packed with the highs, the lows and the quiet moments of each of the first thirty-five milestone years of her life. Her stories are scrapbooked in colors that match the intensity of the life she's led. She document the facts, evaluates her experiences, describes what she's learned, and in the process shows us how much she has grown. Marnie's highs include earning a law degree and becoming a mother. Her lows take us through disappointment, divorce and her life-threatening stroke. Her gentler stories are filled with tales of a loving Canadian childhood. Marnie's album is a joy to look at and a privilege to read.

→

Tag Journaling: I was five when we bought "the boat." A giant old four-door Pontiac. With the new car came a trip to Disneyland. The first 12 hours of driving got us to Salt Lake City. The next 12 to Los Angeles. Rules were strict. No asking how much longer, how much further, how far we have gone. No back seat fighting. No territory disputes. No complaining. And Marnie, please don't throw up. But car sickness was a part of every journey for me. That poor lady at Jack in the Box. Disneyland was wonderful. Warm and sunny. My favorite? The teacups. And, of course, Minnie Mouse.

The first day of school. The first day of the rest of my life. I loved school. From the moment it began. I can still tell you the names of all my 1-12 teachers. A voracious reader, I was no longer limited to the local public library for my daily intake. Additionally I now had monkey bars, field trips, friends, and lessons. A complete pleaser, nothing thrilled me more that seeing a good report card. I learned quickly that being the best had its rewards. Most especially the pride of my dad. He always took time to praise and acknowledge a good grade!

Baker Jr. High had a really great theater program. Each year was a new musical production complete with costumes, makeup, lights, sound. Usually just for students, the year they performed Oliver, they cast some younger siblings to play the parts of the little kids at the orphanage; I got a part! and not just any part. Being the smallest, I was the first on stage for the opening scene; "Is it worth waiting for. . ." The lights, the music, the thrill. Too young to stay for the whole show, I left for home and bed at intermission. Once asleep, I dreamt of being a famous actor one day. My first taste of stardom was absolutely delicious!

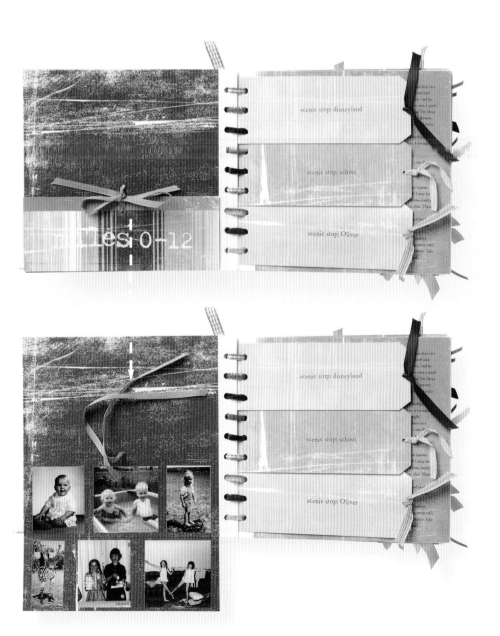

ant old four door
Disneyland. The
e City. The next
sking how much
e gone. No back
omplaining. And
ness was a part of
ck in the Box,
ny. My favorite?
se.

the rest of my life. I
can still tell you the
ous reader, I was no
for my daily intake.
d trips, friends, and
illed me more than
y that being the best
ide of my dad. He
dge a good grade!

ogram. Each year was
h costumes, makeup,
e year they performed
play the parts of the
And not just any part.
for the opening scene.
the music, the thrill.
f for home and bed at
ng a famous actor one
ly delicious!

Mile 0 began about 15 minutes from home in the Lethbridge Regional Hospital. Eleven days late and greeted by two older siblings (Jodi, age 2, and Trevor, age 1) and two parents who were tired and worn out from said two siblings, I was named Monica Jean. This was not to be my actual name, and by the time I went home to Coaldale I had been more appropriately named Marnie Dawn. Home was a small two bedroom home on the outskirts of our town of 5600 people. We stayed in the "little house" for three years, and then relocated to a four level white stucco with black wood trim home in which my parents still live. This house was about four blocks from the first one. At least we began as a very geographically stable family!!

These first 12 miles were relatively utopian. I have the most adoring and adorable mother who felt that her children were golden and we always felt very loved and needed. We had bikes, a swingset, and a canal behind our house for swimming, bug catching, and a taste of nature. My dad taught mathematics and social dancing at RJ Baker Junior High School. My mom began working there as a secretary when I began grade one. Summers were spent camping at Rosen Lake and then at Lake Blaine. That is when we weren't in the field. My Grandma and Grandpa Jorgensen lived on a farm in Iron Springs. We farmed an acre of corn and cucumbers each summer. This meant lots of trips to the farmer's market and hopefully a slurpee on the way home in the back of the little orange Toyota.

Extracurriculars included gymnastics at 3 and 4, then skating from 4 to 7, and piano lessons beginning at mile 5. Highland dancing replaced skating in grade two. Skating made me cold! I may have preferred ballet, but let's not go there. Each summer we took swimming lessons, until everyone finally admitted that taking the same class over and over and over and over was really not the best idea. Then I became the non-swimmer who loved to go the pool every day.

Pets were had only during this period. The kitties went to the farm once they climbed (and snagged) Mom's curtains. The dog was not loved by all, and missed mostly by me when it jumped the fence and was hit by a car. Once its puppies were gone, so were our pets. Not everyone cried.

Saturday mornings were filled with chores, cartoons, and toast with raspberry jam. Sundays mornings were spent in church, followed by a yummy meat and potatoes dinner at the dining room table. Sunday evenings were my favorites, spent watching Donny and Marie, Disney, and being a family. Life was really pretty good. Even with all that orange velvet wallpaper and long golden shag carpet!

our

At mile 17, I had the pleasure of my first big detour. Having decided that I *needed* to attend Harvard, I had completed all the necessary prerequisites. The application had been long and tedious. I had no idea if I would be accepted, but I knew my numbers were good. A recruiter had called a few times and things seemed positive: a female international student with scores to back her up—he told me I was definitely a good candidate. But then without warning, I receive a letter in the mail stating that my application had been terminated as incomplete. Incomplete? What????? Thinking there was some mistake, I promptly called to ask what was missing. I was told that one of my eight letters of recommendation was not there. Mr. Ryan, the guidance counselor, had failed to submit his letter.

In talking to him, Mr. Ryan said that he didn't do his letter as he thought I was kidding about applying to Harvard. So he didn't send it in. With a mere shrug and complete absence of apology, I was expected to understand. Oh, I understood loud and clear. He was lazy. He was incompetent. He had ruined my Harvard dream. And he didn't even care.

Now when you are a kid, you have a pretty good sense that you don't always, or even often, get your way. But you have no idea that adults can completely let you down. And not even apologize. If I had acted that way, there would have been a penalty. But Mr. Ryan just went on his way. It was a bitter realization for someone who thought the world was a pretty kind place.

Thankfully, BYU and the University of Chicago had been my back-up plans. I hurried to make sure that nothing was missing from either of those applications. Not very long after I learned that BYU had accepted me and also given me a full four year (actually five!) tuition scholarship. I accepted and began making plans for Provo, Utah.

I now understand that my life would be completely different had I gone to Boston instead of Provo. Nearly all of my friends came as a result of going to BYU. My choice of profession, my direction, my life—everything I am now is somewhat dependent upon the detour down I-15. I am pleased with my life and how it turned out, though I still wish I had had the chance to attend Harvard. Perhaps one day when I am old and grey, I can be that old lady at the back of the room who gets the best grade in the class as she has nothing else to do with her time. Or maybe not. Either way,

Marnie's Approach

Marnie had much to tell in her album "My First 35 Miles," so it required some planning and special techniques. Stories of a sensitive or intense nature are found in "caution" envelopes, which serve to guide the reader's expectations. Stories of disappointment or sadness are marked with "detour" signs.

My first trial was a shoplifting case. My client was homeless and accused of stealing $33.00 of supplies from a local food store. More than a bit mentally ill, he refused to accept the plea, though he admitted his guilt. Preparing for trial over a holiday weekend in July, 1998, I entered court ready to fight a good losing battle. Judge Peuler presided over our jury trial. The jury returned an unsurprising guilty verdict, though we celebrated the outcome as a victory. The offer had included a recommendation for 2 weeks jail time, Judge Peuler only imposed one. So, in fact, we did better by going to trial. My first lesson at LDA? Find the small victories. There will be few big ones.

Trying to decide when to have a baby is a bit tricky for me. The notion that I feel mature enough for such a responsibility seems egomaniacal. So I was grateful when it just kind of happened. Richard and I were thrilled with the prospect of being parents, though worried about financially supporting a child. Funny thing is that somehow it just sort of all works out. That's the benefit of paying one's tithing. Nigel Quincy was born December 23, 1998. With swirly dark hair and piercingly dark eyes, we fell in love at an instant. He was healthy and handsome and captured me unlike anything before. I loved him with everything I am. Instantly. How startling. How incredible.

The LSAT is an admissions test for law schools around the nation. It is offered four times a year, and most students now take a review class to help them conquer the exam. I stumbled onto a teaching position during my first year of law school at Kaplan Test Center. Little did I know then that this would support us for many years. After Kaplan, I taught at BYU, eventually redesigning their entire course. I love teaching. The students are attentive as the class is quite expensive, and they really want the help—a wonderful environment. Generally happy to avoid the spotlight, standing in front of a class transforms me. Funny, irreverent, happy to be there. I love teaching.

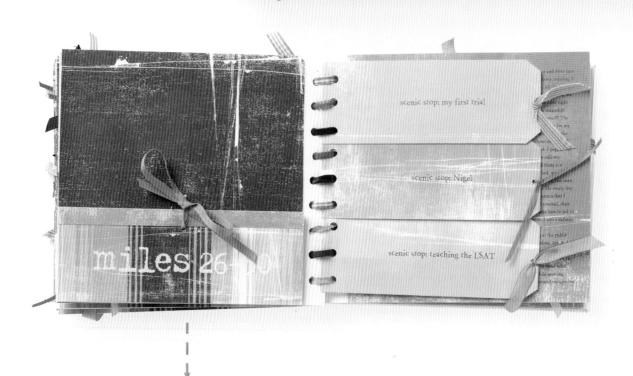

scenic stop: my first trial

scenic stop: Nigel

scenic stop: teaching the LSAT

miles 26-30

Picking up the pieces is something I do well. So I told no one of my shameful failure and dove into my job as a law clerk bailiff for Judge Thorne. Having received the first half of Police Academy training, I now received extra training from the sheriff's office. Becoming weapon certified was great. My first target was 4 shots out of 50. The rangemaster came over to watch me to see why I was soooo bad. Smacking me on the head with his clipboard, he told me to close the other eye. Apparently I was trying to shoot right handed and left eyed! The trouble is, I am so left eye dominant that I couldn't do it. With a makeshift cardboard patch made from an ammo box, my next target was 48 out of 50. What a sharpshooter!!! The rangemaster took such a liking to me and my skill that he fixed me up with a special gun. Smaller for my girly hands and with an easier trigger pull for my delicate fingers. However good a shooter I was on the range, at the courthouse, I usually left my gun in the locker. Too much of a liability without my patch!!

Being a bailiff was interesting. I liked my white socks over the black they suggested. I pegged the legs on my pants and left my shirt open one button too many. I obviously didn't belong in a military environment. Though my bosses Sargent Chard and Lieutenant Marx were incredible. And there is a certain kick that comes with wearing a sheriff's uniform. On the other hand, being a law clerk was wonderful. Good hours. Great learning. Working for Judge Thorne was second to none. A kind, fair man with immense compassion. In the two years I worked for him, I learned many great lessons. He rarely lost his temper and always gave consideration to the defense. After my mile 26 failure, I was certain that I could still be a prosecutor. However, I found myself relating more and more to the defense counsel, their fervor, their arguments. I also had tears in my eyes as I had to handcuff a 16-year-old to take him to jail to begin his one-year sentence. This mirror was too great. I was not meant to be a prosecutor. I was a defense attorney in my soul. Strange how little I know myself sometimes.

They say if you want to learn the war, you go to the trenches, so I began applying at the public defenders' office. After a year and a half of applying to Salt Lake Legal Defenders' Association, Mr. F. John Hill finally hired me. It was there in those trenches that I found my true calling. Hired mid-mile 26, I spent a mere half mile in the misdemeanor division. With just a few trials under my belt, I was moved to the felony division after returning from having had Nigel. Here I was able to give a voice to those who needed one, to hold the system accountable, to help people who really needed help. All while wearing heels, suits, and scarves. I couldn't have asked for more. I was loving my amazing and profound occupation!

Journaling is the first focus of Marnie's album, with photos featured as small, hidden treasures. Untie a ribbon here or turn over a brightly patterned tag there to find the photos. This technique helps stop Marnie's scrapbook from being too information-dense and overwhelming.

caution

Why my smooth life was brutally interrupted by a stroke is not something anyone can easily explain. One minute I am a wife and mother climbing the professional ladder. The next I am lying in a bed that will not stop spinning as I eavesdrop on nurses unabashedly talking of death, paralysis, and bladder bags. (I can hear you, I want to scream, but yet, I cannot.) Though people around me try to explain what is going on, nothing sinks in. Just random thoughts. One. Thrilled to be alive. Two. Guilt for still being kept alive. Three. Panic. Why was I spared? Why me? Four. Anger. Why me? Why at all? Stupid me for not just driving home. Five. Tired. I'm just sooo tired. Six. Pain. My head hurts. Could everyone please just stand still? Seven. Relief. My mom is here. Eight. Guilt. My mom had to come. Nine. Shhh. Please everyone, just be quiet and sit still. Ten. Gratitude. For being alive. For a family that is standing by me. For a second chance. Lastly, overwhelm. How will this affect me?

Truth is, having a stroke changed everything. Foremost, I relinquished control. I learned that one cannot plan for everything and that I am not in control of my life. To believe so is an egomaniacal thought that eliminates God from the equation. Lesson two, family matters. Friends matter. It is really all about the people in our lives. Not the money, status, trophies, accomplishments. Lesson three, bad things happen to good people. God cannot keep bad things from happening to us, but He can help ease our pain and suffering. Lesson four, life is fragile. I am, too. I have limits and I cannot conquer the world in one day, or maybe even one lifetime. And that's okay. Lesson five, listen to your body. Eat if you are hungry. Sleep if you are tired. Sit down when you are dizzy. Respect your physical boundaries. The price is steep if you don't. Lesson six, always keep a clean kitchen floor. I cannot believe how dirty my house was when my family rolled in. How embarrassing. Lesson seven, it doesn't matter if your floor is dirty. Lesson eight, simplify. Your life, your home, your obligations. Don't run faster than you should. Lesson nine, healing takes time. And finally, lesson ten, some why's have no good answer. Sometimes you go on living just because you are alive. Don't spend too much time seeking answers to elusive questions. God is allowed His mysteries and we are allowed trials of our faith.

I would be lying if I said that I was glad to have had my stroke. (I'm actually embarrassed that Heavenly Father apparently has to take such drastic measures to teach me my lessons!!) That said, my stroke affected my life so pervasively that I cannot imagine where we would be had I not had it. All the big decisions we have made since then have had to be affected by it. Where we live. How we live. Activities. Jobs. Schedules. Many little decisions also cannot be made without thinking of my limitations. Are there ceiling fans? Will it be too noisy or too busy? Life is as it is. Different than it would have been obviously, but not entirely all bad. Family is first, now. Always. Food and sleep are treasured. Heavenly Father is to be consulted often. And life is rarely taken for granted.

Scrapbooking Your Self-Discovery Album

Self-discovery albums are made for many reasons. Perhaps you wish to preserve a record of your life before you became a parent or left college. Maybe you want to leave your children a legacy of lessons learned. You may want to use a self-discovery album to help you sort out what's important in your life or to number the things you're grateful for. Writing about yourself may be the last thing you've thought of doing, but it may be one of the most important.

To make a self-discovery album of your own, try one of the techniques used in this chapter of **Scrapbooks to Cherish.** Ask yourself, as Mou Saha did, what you would want to share with your children should you ever be faced with a life-threatening illness? Try Jennifer Adams Donnelly's 30 Reasons to Love My Life: Where I've Been, Who I Am and What I Want to Do. Or, use Marnie Flores' milestone organization—using a mile for each year and mile markers or detours for important events.

Here are some additional ideas to help you write your own story:

My past, present and future

10 things I know for sure

My childhood memories

My hometown

My favorite things

A day in my life

What I've learned

Random facts about me

My senior year

These are a few of my favorite things

A self-discovery album is similar to a tribute album, except it is about you, so you may also find useful ideas in the tribute section.

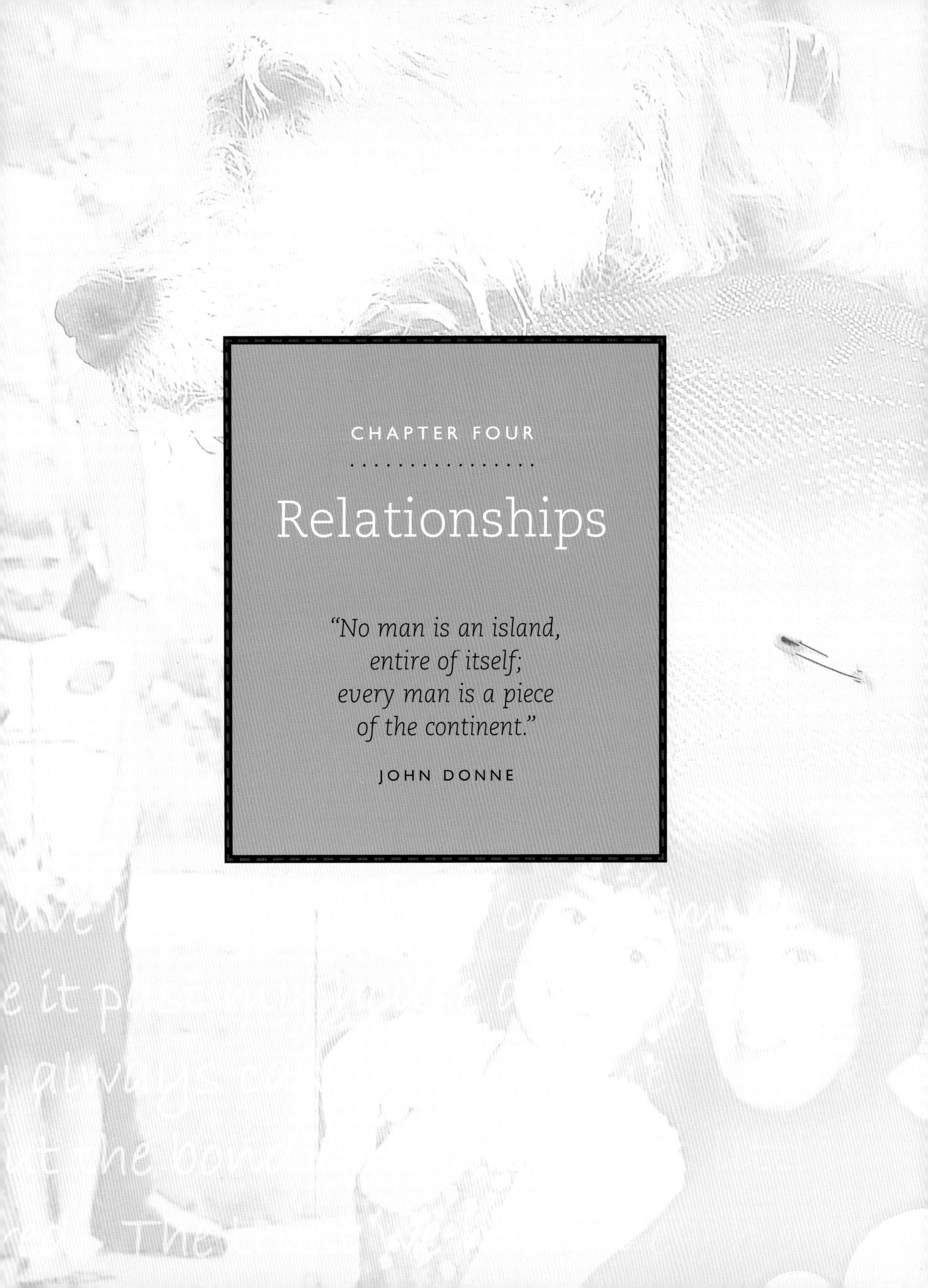

. . . .

CHAPTER FOUR

Relationships

"No man is an island,
entire of itself;
every man is a piece
of the continent."

JOHN DONNE

The winning relationship albums are full of personal and moving stories that describe strong and loving bonds. We all had tears in our eyes when we read about **Sarah Doyle** and her mother who had always been everything to  each other, and then were separated by hundreds of miles. Sarah's album caught our hearts for the sheer intensity of her love for her mother and her mother's commitment to her. We bet you too find tears in your eyes when you read through this beautiful album.

People are not the only ones we grow to love. Who wouldn't fall in love with **Kendra Wietstock's** precious doggy friend, Baby? And who wouldn't grieve  with her when Baby lost her fight with cancer? This album touched our hearts and reminded us of how much it means to have a pet's unconditional love in our lives.

The unqualified love of a father was another of our winning relationship albums. We chose **JoAnne Hoatson's**

 album because it reflected family life and love, in all its varied forms. Some of JoAnne's journaling about her father is deeply meaningful, and some of it is simply hilarious. This full and honest look at family dynamics made JoAnne's album a winner for us.

The relationship album winners recognized and documented deep and loving feelings in their scrapbooks. Be sure you have tissues close by as we share their heartfelt albums with you.

"You are so much more than my mother—you are my forever friend. Life has found us miles apart and I continue to battle the sadness in my heart. It is a void that no other can fill. I am grateful for all of our memories and of course for the countless photographs and phone calls that help me remain close to you. I will visit every chance I get and I know you will do the same. I remember lying on the beach with you last summer, holding your hand and wishing I could stay. I knew in a few days I would have to say goodbye—a pain that would last long after I left Florida. Anticipation for our second visit is high, yet in the back of my mind I know the days will pass quickly and wonder how long it will be until I see you again. I miss you already Mom. I love you. Sarah."

Across the years Sarah and her mother were there for each other—just the two of them. Then came her mother's wrenching move to Florida, hundreds of miles away.

Sarah's decision to make this album came a year after her mother moved to Florida, and Sarah began planning a Christmas vacation to visit her. What Sarah originally envisioned as a great Christmas present instead became a deep and emotional journey exploring her mother's role in her life. It also helped heal the wounds of separation inflicted by the miles between them.

Sarah's album was a gift to recognize, honor, and most of all, thank her mother for a lifetime of love and dedication! The lasting memory book that resulted is the story of their bond and a gift her mother treasures.

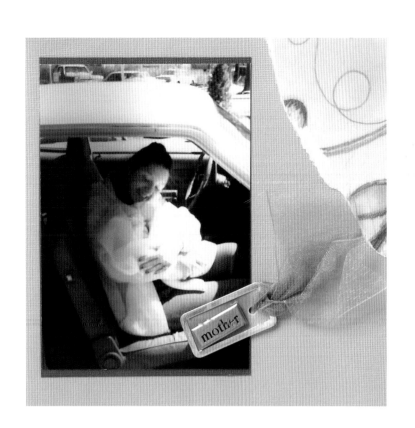

Mom

This album is my gift to you for a lifetime of love sacrifice and treasured memories that belong to only you and I. Thank you for being a strong hard-working and devoted woman who I am proud to call my mother. This is my story of us just the two of us. Each page is a glimpse into the unconditional role you held as my mother. nurturer, provider, teacher, protector, motivator, confidant, and friend

I am forever grateful

All my love Sarah

Sarah's Approach

Sarah's small album did not need heavy embell-ishment, which would have overpowered the all-important journaling. In such a heartfelt project, the thank-you notes from Sarah to her mother are most important elements in the album. To give consistency to the pages and make them more attractive, Sarah used small pieces of the same rose-patterned paper over green cardstock on each page. Notes are pinned to the cardstock with miniature safety pins. Small ribbons, metal tags and buttons complete the page.

motherhood

I leaned on you consistently my first year as a mother and even more so when I married Shane. I was beginning a new family and leaving behind the only life I knew me and you. I faced many challenges and turned to you for support advice and reassurance. Motherhood is a system of trial and error and all the books I read could not have prepared me for what lay ahead. It is also the most rewarding of any of my accomplishments. Thank you for your unconditional listening and for not being judgemental. Your honest insight might not have always been what I wanted to hear but I know you care and I'm glad I have you to confide in

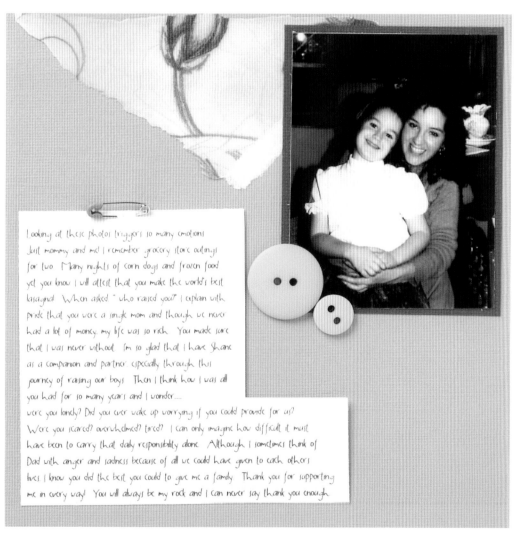

Looking at these photos triggers so many emotions. Just mommy and me! I remember grocery store outings for two. Many nights of corn dogs and frozen food, yet you know I will attest that you make the world's best lasagna! When asked "who raised you?" I explain with pride that you were a single mom and though we never had a lot of money, my life was so rich. You made sure that I was never without. I'm so glad that I have Shane as a companion and partner especially through this journey of raising our boys. Then I think how I was all you had for so many years and I wonder...

Were you lonely? Did you ever wake up worrying if you could provide for us? Were you scared? overwhelmed? tired? I can only imagine how difficult it must have been to carry that daily responsibility alone. Although I sometimes think of Dad with anger and sadness because of all we could have given to each others lives. I know you did the best you could to give me a family. Thank you for supporting me in every way! You will always be my rock and I can never say thank you enough.

my wish for you...

Mom

In conclusion I want you to know that above all
I want you to be happy. I know in my heart
that you miss me that you miss all of us, but
I also know that you made a decision that was
best for you and your family. I don't think we
knew how truly difficult it would be to live this
far apart. I want you to enjoy the warm winters
that you longed for and who knows what the
future holds for us! Some things will never change
like the happiness you've given me and the love and
support I will always have for you where ever we may be!
I love you Mom
-Sarah

My Precious Friend

Author Unknown

I Love you with all my heart.
Each Day you greet me with such affection
And unconditional love.
I will never betray your trust.
You will always have
My best care and attention.
Some say you may not have a soul,
But when I look into
Your big beautiful brown eyes,
I know in my heart
That God has prepared
A special place For You.

Baby
June 3, 1989
To
May 7, 2003

Many pets are waiting patiently with Baby at the Rainbow Bridge.

Pets are often the miracle glue that helps hold our lives together. Their companionship lifts our lives, and their unconditional love and trust make us better people. What better way to remember special pet relationships than to scrapbook their stories and honor their loving personalities and playful ways. "My Precious Friend, Baby" does just that.

"This album is a remembrance of a special bond I shared with my little dog, Baby. She struggled with cancer for two years before she died. Even now, almost a year after her death, I sit here crying as I recall her last day. This album was a way for me to say goodbye."

Kendra's Approach

Kendra used a watermark ink to stamp delightful paw prints on each caramel-colored cardstock page. She used black cardstock as a frame for each page, and offers this hint. "I cut out the centers of the black background cardstock and used them to mat the photos. Once the caramel-colored cardstock was attached on each side, you couldn't tell there were holes in the backgrounds. It saved on the amount of cardstock needed and made the book lighter."

Dedication

This book is dedicated to my wonderful friend, Baby. You were so courageous and strong and you will live in my heart forever.

Ever since I can remember, I have had a dog or a cat in my life. Stray pets never seem to make it past my house and those sweet faces at the Humane Society always called my name. I have had so many special pets, but the bond I had with this little terrier mutt, cannot be compared. The trust we had in each other was amazing. I always knew before anyone else, when she wasn't feeling well and she always knew when I needed to cuddle. At the very end of her two-year struggle with cancer, she died in my arms. As hard as that was for me, there is no other place I could have been but with her. It took almost a year before I could put this book together & I cried like crazy when I wrote Baby's cancer story. However, this book helped me say goodbye to my dear little furry friend, Baby.

Baby, look for me by the Rainbow Bridge.

Love, Kendra

I LOVE YOU

How Baby Joined Our Family

When Baby was 2 ½ years old, we adopted her from the Elkhart County Humane Society. We were volunteering at an Adopt-A-Pet at Concord Mall. I fell in love with her the moment I saw her in the cage at the shelter. After the Adopt-A-Pet, it took everything in me NOT to take her home that instant. Unfortunately, 3 different families put a hold on Baby that day. We decided to put a hold on her too. Well our friends at the Humane Society bypassed the other holds and decided to place her with us. I will always be grateful for that act of kindness. Because she was brought to the shelter with vet tags on, we were able to find out some limited information about her health, including her birthday, June 3, 1989 (our wedding anniversary) and that she had already been spayed.

She fit right into our family from the start & was a wonderful dog. She was very skiddish, especially when Tim read the newspaper. We think her previous owners had mistreated her. They got rid of her because they were having a baby. She and Jessica (our Golden Retriever) got along right away. They played and slept together all the time. Baby was with Jessica right before Jessie died. Baby just seemed to know what was going on. She wasn't too crazy about Kayla our new Golden puppy. After about a week, they started playing & got along great. Baby wasn't crazy about the Megan & Matthew either. Sometimes they would chase her & make lots of noise; however, she was always very good with them. She didn't mind them as much the last few years, only because she was completely deaf. Oh, one more thing about Baby – she was a bed hog!

Baby had a wonderful life with us & we were blessed to have her with us so long. She fought over 2 years with cancer & died on May 7, 2003 (27 days short of her 14th birthday).

GIRLFRIENDS

The Rainbow Bridge

Author unknown

There is a bridge connecting Heaven and Earth. It is called the Rainbow Bridge because of its many colors. Just this side of the Rainbow Bridge there is a land of meadows, hills & valleys with lush green grass. When a beloved pet dies, the pet goes to this place. There is always food & water and warm spring weather. The old & frail animals are young again. They play all day with each other. There is only one thing missing. They are not with their special person who loved them on Earth.

So, each day they run and play until the day comes when one suddenly stops playing and looks up! The nose twitches, the ears are up, the eyes are staring and this one suddenly runs from the group. You have been seen, and when you and your special friend meet, you take her in your arms & embrace. Your face is kissed again and again and again, and you look once more into the eyes of your trusting pet. Then you cross the Rainbow Bridge together, never again to be separated.

Baby's Last photograph • May 3, 2003 • IN her favorite chair ♥♥♥

DOGS PRAYER

Now I lay me down to sleep,
The Queen size bed is soft and deep.
I sleep right in the center groove,
My human being can hardly move.
I've trapped her legs, She's tucked in tight
And here is where I pass the night.
No one disturbs me or does intrude,
Till morning comes and "I want food!"
I sneak up slowly to begin,
And nibble on my humans chin.
For the morning is here, And it's time to play.
I always seem to get my way.
So thank you Lord for giving me,
This human person that I see.
The one who hugs me and holds me tight,
And shares her bed with me at night.

Poem by Thena Smith
CK Message Board

The one absolutely **unselfish** friend that man can have is his dog

Do you have a photo of your dad riding a girl's bike? JoAnne does.

The focus of JoAnne's album "Dad, What I Learned" is her relationship with her father and the life lessons he taught her. Some of the lessons learned are deeply meaningful, and some reflect the lighter side of family life. From him JoAnne learned, "It's not days we remember, it's moments," as well as "We are the only normal family," and that "As long as your family are alive they will embarrass you."

"I created this album for my Dad for Father's Day. He has been a tremendous influence on my life. The dedication page says, "This book is dedicated to my DAD, who taught me how to live, laugh, and to love."
This album reflects each of those aspects. Dad has always loved my mother deeply, and he has a zest for life that he has passed on to me, my siblings and his grandchildren. He can find humor in everyday life, and can laugh at himself. Each page of this album was crafted with love."

I learned that...

It's not days
we remember,
it's moments.

JoAnne's Approach

JoAnne snuck her family albums from her parents' home and scanned every picture into her computer. She printed out the pictures that she wanted to use in this album and made her Dad pose for a couple of additional pictures, without telling him what they were for. JoAnne didn't use all the scanned photos in this album. Those that remain on her computer will be a wonderful resource for future albums and a family legacy JoAnne will be glad she took time to preserve.

If you don't have the time to scan all of Mom and Dad's old photos, there are many reputable services that will do the job for you. Do a Web search for "photo scanning." We found many services that offer to scan 100 photos for around $35-45.

CHRISTMAS 1971

I learned that...

As long as you are holding hands, you are never very far apart.

Cherish the memories you have. Good and the bad. The good times bring you happiness, and the bad ones build your character.

The more memories you have, the better you'll remember those who are close to you.

D S W A V O H P J E Z B N Y I L R E

I learned that.....

the best
thing to
spend
on kids
is time

Dad,
there are two
lasting gifts
you've given
me.
One is Roots,
the other is
Wings.

Thank you

A relationship album is similar to a tribute album but instead of focusing on your family member, friend or pet, the focus is on two people and the nature of their relationship. Choosing a narrower focus of time or activity, as one of our authors did, allows you to tell the story in a clearer and more heartfelt way.

Themes for Your Relationship Album

The albums featured in this chapter of **Scrapbooks to Cherish,** describe relationships with a father—JoAnne Hoatson's "Dad, What I Learned" filled with both tongue-in-cheek and earnest family wisdom; with a pet—Kendra Wietstock's "My Precious Friend, Baby" describing her much-loved dog's fight with cancer; and with a mother—Sarah Doyle's "Mom and Me" in which Sarah uses the distance that separates them as a magnifying glass for their relationship. Here are some other theme ideas you might consider as you reflect on a special relationship you enjoy with another and would like to document:

The day I spent with you

Things I love most about you

My childhood memories of you

He says, she says

The summer I spent with you

Me and my shadow

The sacrifices you made for me

Stories of our childhood

From your friends and family

What I would tell you if you were here today

Your letters and cards (or emails)

Doing chores with you

Two peas in a pod

How I'm like you and why that's good

Like mother, like daughter; or like father, like son

. . . .

CHAPTER FIVE

Journey

"May your trails be crooked,
winding, lonesome, dangerous,
leading to the most amazing view.
May your mountains rise into
and above the clouds."

EDWARD ABBEY

For most of us, vacation memories are some of our richest. We're relaxed. We're seeing new sights, hearing new sounds. Perhaps we're eating unfamiliar and interesting food. And, we're often spending more time than we usually do with family and friends. Travel is a way of learning about something different from our day-to-day world, while building shared memories and stronger relationships.

These themes are scrapbooked in abundance in the winning albums of the Journey category of the "Coolest Album Ever" contest.

Elizabeth Dillow's album documents a trip that was originally planned to give her a weekend away from her day-to-day child-rearing responsibilities. What her journey, and consequent album, becomes is an artistic and poetic feast for the eyes and heart. What Elizabeth shows us through her trip to Santa Fe is this: "The real voyage of discovery consists not of seeing new landscapes, but in having new eyes."

Sheila Doherty's winning album captures the bittersweet feelings of two friends and their children spending three last days together before life takes them in different directions. Sheila's album is packed with the story of six small children, six car seats, a Ford Expedition, two very tired moms and lots of love.

Cory Richardson-Lauve's album describes how much she and her family loved the laughter and all the silly vacation stories they shared while seeing San Francisco together. Their journey makes a wonderful framework for an album that describes the trip and the deeper family connections that were forged in those few days.

Let's open the albums of our Journey winners and travel with them as they get away from it all and surround themselves with beauty, history, friends and family.

"If art is the one way possible of speaking truth, then I witnessed more verity in two and a half days than many people see in a lifetime. Santa Fe is synonymous with art: every possible available inch of real estate in the town that is not devoted to the fabulous food held so much canvas, fabric, mixed media and photo paper that it was liable to burst at the seams from all the creativity. If and when I have the opportunity to return to Santa Fe, many of those artists will have packed up their personal masterpieces and set up shop in another gallery in another city. Most will never rise to the level of fame of Jackson Pollock, Andy Warhol, or Georgia O'Keefe, but they will most definitely remain for me as an inspiration to live creatively."

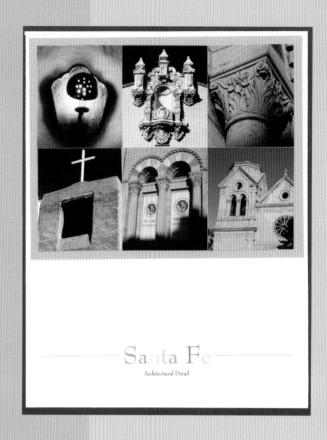

For Elizabeth, Santa Fe felt like leaving the United States and entering an exciting foreign country.

Elizabeth Dillow's album "Santa Fe: A City Different," allows us to see a colorful and historic cityscape through her appreciative eyes. Her journey, which was originally planned as a weekend away from a newly weaned daughter, turns into an energetic celebration of art, architecture, color, culture and the enduring nature of life itself.

I took this trip as a celebration, albeit a bittersweet one.

The plot was hatched many months earlier as Maddie turned one year old. I knew that I couldn't continue nursing her forever, despite the fact that neither of us was particularly ready to give it up. I surprised myself at how much I enjoyed the nursing experience; it was certainly not the aspect of having a baby that interested me most before Maddie was born. Suddenly, however, our nursing days seemed to be numbered and it left me anxious in a way I had never before experienced. I decided that what I needed was a weekend away—something fun to distract me as well as a clean break from nursing. Matt agreed that this was probably the best course of action; I hadn't yet been away from Maddie for more than an afternoon or evening, and he was more than happy to have a weekend alone with Maddie without me around to remind him of things he hadn't forgotten to do.

I approached Jill with the idea of a weekend trip and after a summer of life-altering changes of her own, she readily agreed to the plan. Though I wanted to go in August when Maddie turned 15 months old, we were unable to coordinate our schedules to make it work that month. I chose to stop nursing on the day Maddie turned 15 months anyway, substituting an early morning photography trip to Garden of the Gods instead of my grand plan to hit the open road. Isn't this what I wanted—to be free from my responsibilities from time to time? I struggled with my choice, even though it was a sound decision: I had nursed Maddie a full nine months longer than my original goal, and I was proud of that commitment. Maddie survived the day with good cheer;
why was it such a difficult day for me?

It was obvious that a celebration was still in order.

So I continued to research and plan a trip. I decided Santa Fe was the perfect destination; not too far (five hours) to visit by car for a weekend. I'd never been to New Mexico, but hearing descriptions of the city from other friends had always transfixed me. Jill and I finally pinned down a weekend to make our trip: a crisp fall weekend in October. As the date to leave approached, I got more and more nervous; how could I possibly leave my daughter overnight? Over a weekend? Over state lines? What if something happened to me? Never much for worrying about travel, I suddenly became consumed with worries totally foreign to me. I summoned all my bravery and repeated to myself how much I had earned this trip. I wanted a weekend to be free of the daily responsibilities of child-rearing; to travel to a place that had grown to mythical proportions in my imagination; to reconnect with Jill after a whirlwind summer; to rediscover my passion for photography.

And so I packed my bags, loaded the car, and started on my journey.

This is what I saw.

Canyon Road
Santa Fe, New Mexico
October 2003

ANDREW SMITH GALLERY, INC.

HERMAN LEONARD

ANDREW SMITH GALLERY, INC.
Masterpieces of 19th and 20th Century Photography

203 W. San Francisco St   Tel: (505) 984-1234
Santa Fe, NM 87501   Fax: (505) 983-2428
www.AndrewSmithGallery.com
Andrew@AndrewSmithGallery.com

the real thing

amazing

Elizabeth's Approach

Elizabeth's album mimics the texture and color of the adobe walls she saw in Santa Fe. To do this, she used the easy-to-duplicate technique of stamping her entire stamp pad directly onto Kraft or earth-toned cardstock. The photos in this album are art pieces in themselves. To prevent detailed journaling from overwhelming them, Elizabeth has sewn pockets on to the bottom of several pages. Additional journaling as well as brochures, maps and other travel memorabilia are tucked in each pocket.

I've never seen a city so distinct in character as Santa Fe... the color, texture, size, and placement of each structure in the parts of town we wandered in were like no other. There are scores of different shades and textures of adobe, ever-changing throughout the day depending upon the sunlight. The shops, museums, and restaurants seemed to be working in concordance with the land and each other so much more than more traditional city structures of steel and brick. At first glance the streets looked similar as Jill and I followed them, under the advice of the *Off the Beaten Path* book, with no particular agenda. But when the city is walked at a leisurely pace, the quirks and beauty appear much more strongly. Burros painted on the sides of buildings... tiny slits for windows that keep out the heat... white, weathered crosses standing proudly atop truly old churches...The feeling of leaving the United States and entering a foreign country hovered over me for much of our adventure; how exciting it is to realize that this country is so diverse despite the strip malls and chain restaurants. Even those establishments were unlike what I'm used to seeing: adobe fast food joints and low-slung discount stores marked the landscape of the boundaries of Santa Fe, just far enough outside the old parts of town not to ruin the essence of it all. I think it was Will Rogers who said something to the effect that Santa Fe was designed by drunkards riding backwards on donkeys. This may be a bit harsh, but it is a city that demands a slower pace, an adventurous spirit, and an eye for detail.

Somewhere between Santa Fe & Taos...

→

Journaling: While walking on Canyon Road, these orange berries growing along the sidewalks and next to adobe buildings caught my attention nearly as much as the galleries we visited. Against the turquoise of the window frames and filtered through the mid-afternoon light, they absolutely glowed. Orange is a difficult color for me to describe; spicy reds, cheerful yellows, and fresh greens are so much easier to decipher. Orange is the color of flowers, fire, fall and a favorite shirt from J. Crew I used to own before it wore out from too much use. It is a surprising color, appearing with a jolt out of a sea of more acceptable hues. When orange is overused it can be overwhelming and downright hideous. Maybe that is why I like how much magic a dash of orange possesses; it reminds me of the beauty of subtlety in nature that demands a second look.

Journaling:

Once more the liberal year laughs out
O'er richer stores than gems of gold;
Once more with harvest song and shout
Is nature's boldest triumph told.
—JOHN GREENLEAF WHITTIER, "HARVEST HYMN"

While visiting San Ildefonso, we asked around for a more scenic route back home than the interstate. The man who owned the studio where Jill bought her pottery recommended a back way to Taos and then on through northern New Mexico and southern Colorado until we met up with I-25 again at Walsenburg. We were just thrilled to find Sopyn's Market along the way. We almost didn't stop—in fact, the market came up so fast along the two lane highway that we actually passed it at first and had to turn around. We couldn't have asked for a better surprise; one of our favorite things to do together is to explore farmer's markets. The sky was stunningly blue that morning and the items for sale were bursting with the browns, golds, oranges, and deep reds of fall. The elderly woman who owned the market proudly showed us the wreaths and other arrangements she made each year by hand. It was so difficult to pick just one—I'd never seen an arrangement like hers before. The mixtures of dried chili peppers and flowers, wheat, raffia, and gourds were authentic New Mexico through and through. After wandering around taking pictures of pumpkins and peppers, we each finally chose a wreath to purchase—along with some apples for the trip. The advice from the tour book about finding the best places while looking for nothing in particular held true once again. It was definitely one of the highlights of the trip.

→

Journaling: My trip to Santa Fe was a celebration and I accomplished what I set out to do: I explored, photographed, absorbed, and savored the beauty of this southwestern city. I rekindled a valued friendship and I exercised a bit of independence, just to be sure that I still had some. Yet driving home on that Sunday afternoon, I was anxious as I marveled at the fiery aspen spilling down the mountain sides: I was ready to be home. When I walked in the door to a dinner just ready to be put on the table by my husband and a huge bear hug from my little girl, I knew I was exactly where I belonged. It's good to get away, but it's even better to be home.

Orange

outside the Artist's Cafe
· Canyon Road ·

time to go

My trip to Santa Fe was a celebration and I accomplished what I set out to do: I explored, photographed, absorbed, and savored the beauty of this southwestern city. I rekindled a valued friendship and I exercised a bit of independence, just to be sure that I still had some. Yet driving home on that Sunday afternoon, I was anxious as I marveled at the fiery aspen spilling down the mountainsides: I was ready to be home. When I walked in the door to a dinner just ready to be put on the table by my husband and a huge bear hug from my little girl, I knew I was exactly where I belonged. It's good to get away, but it's even better to be home.

"If I'd have known that we would be leaving California, I know I would have done things differently.

We definitely would have gone to the beach more often. These photos are bittersweet snapshots of moments that aren't to come again very soon. Even harder than leaving the beaches behind is leaving behind our best friends."

Two tired moms, six small children, six car seats, one Ford Expedition and two deeply connected families are the subject of Sheila Doherty's album.

"Some people come into our lives, leaving footprints on our hearts, never to be the same," notes Sheila in her album "3 Days." For Sheila and her children, leaving their friends the Brouwers was much harder than leaving the beaches of California. Sheila's husband and the furniture had gone on ahead, so she and her children camped out at the Brouwers for three days before joining him. Those last emotional days were spent on day trips to several of the children's favorite places. This album was made to commemorate the friends' final three days together.

Oceanside PIER

Can 6 kids in carseats and 2 moms fit in a Ford Expedition? Yes, they can! It's a tight fit, but we proved it could be done on our last 3 days together. After over 2 years of meeting at parks, zoos and playgrounds several times a week, our time was quickly coming to an end with our move to Idaho. With Joel headed off to Idaho with the moving truck, we stayed with our best friends, the Brouwers, for our last days in California. We weren't sure how we'd manage it, sleeping over for 2 nights, but we wanted to spend as much time together so we could before the kids and I took off for our new home.

The last moments together were bittersweet for Shannon and I as we watched our kids play together for what would be the last time for a long time. I know I had tears in my eyes on many occasions as Rebekah and Haley splashed in the water at the beach or Erick and Luke held hands in play. Even seeing Jonathon take his first of many steps made my heart ache, knowing that we were going to have to say goodbye.

July 20 - Oceanside Pier
July 21 - Swimming Hole
July 22 - Boomers Kidopolis

We only spent three hours at the beach. With six small children and only two adults, it's understandable. Of the three hours, Beka and Haley spent 10 minutes of it on the playground and the rest of it in the water. In and out with the crashing of the waves. Not even building a sandcastle with their brothers would tempt them out of the water.

Luke was a bit of a loner on this trip. With a small truck in hand (as usual), he made tracks pushing it through the wet sand. He didn't mind the waves too much, but if they got too big, he'd run ashore. At one point he lost his truck to the waves and it took the help of some children down shore to retrieve it and return it to him.

As for Erick, I have never seen a child so afraid of the waves. Getting wet was fine, but as soon as a wave would come, Erick was two steps ahead of it on the shore. He spent more time digging in the sand by his mother's side than in the water.

Jonathon, of course, thought sand was something to be tasted and savored. Half the time he was shoveling sand into a bucket and the other half into his mouth. He enjoyed the water much more than his big brother, giggling wildly as his mommy held him up so the waves would tickle his feet.

Tyler enjoyed his very first trip to the beach in Mommy's arms. He was hypnotized by the waves and delighted watching the children playing in them. All the noise and excitement eventually lulled him to sleep. It was a very relaxing visit for him.

When it came time to leave, there were many protests. Once in the truck though, Luke was asleep in his carseat before the truck had even left the parking lot. Beka soon followed suit.

← **Journaling:** Can 6 kids in carseats and 2 moms fit in a Ford Expedition? Yes they can! It's a tight fit, but we proved it could be done on our last 3 days together. After over 2 years of meeting at parks, zoos and playgrounds several times a week, our time was quickly coming to an end with our move to Idaho. With Joel headed off to Idaho with the moving truck, we stayed with our best friends, the Brouwers, for our last days in California. We weren't sure how we'd manage it, sleeping over for 2 nights, but we wanted to spend as much time together as we could before the kids and I took off for our new home.

The last moments together were bittersweet for Shannon and I as we watched our kids play together for what would be the last time for a long time. I know I had tears in my eyes on many occasions as Rebekah and Haley splashed in the water at the beach or Erick and Luke held hands in play. Even seeing Jonathon take his first of many steps made my heart ache, knowing that we were going to have to say goodbye.

HAPPINESS walks on busy feet. ~Kittie Turmell

Sheila's Approach

No two page layouts in Sheila's album
are the same design. This often leaves a
smaller, project-type album feeling disconnected.
Why doesn't that happen in Sheila's album "3 Days."?
It doesn't happen because Sheila uses one strong design
element—the circle—to tie photos, journaling, paper and
embellishments together on every single page! Much of the
background paper is dotted. The photos are cut into circles.
Embellishments are circular metal. The journaling is inside a
circle or run alongside the edge of a circle. Even some of the
children's photos were taken in a circular swimming pool
or framed in the circular openings of the playground
equipment. Despite the many photo locations and
multiple subjects, Sheila's use of the circle as a
strong and consistent design element
helps unify her varied pages.

"I created this album to document our trip to San Francisco. I especially want to remember the fun that we had, the sights we saw, and the connections between my family members that the trip helped strengthen. I am dedicating the album to the members of my family who have taught me to seek adventure and laugh along the way."

San Francisco

APRIL 2004

There are moments in life when a particular decision leads to an experience you will never forget. For Cory and her family, a taxi cab ride was one of these moments.

Cory Richardson-Lauve's album "San Francisco" documents the love and laughter her family shared while seeing San Francisco together. The album reflects this merriment and is full of amusing journaling like the following: "The Pacifica. We detested this member of our traveling party and it hardly deserves a page in the book. It certainly deserves no fancy fonts, embellishments, colorful paper or careful cropping. Its cave-like interior boasted room for six passengers, but did not serve them all equally, with passengers in the rear relying on accounts from the front seat passengers in order to take in the scenery." And in a description of Fisherman's Wharf: "A swift walk through included sea lions yelping and tourists yelping louder."

JAPANESE TEA garden

THE CONSERVATORY

Journaling: We quickly obtained our goods (a mostly fixed camera) and continued on to gaze at a variety of plants at the newly reconstructed conservatory. We were somewhat hampered by the lack of identifying labels on the unusual flowers and plants, but enjoyed the variety of displays.

We then continued west into the foggy Richmond district for the dim sum at Tom Kiangs. While the dishes' names were hard to understand, they were easy to gobble down. Even the more skeptical diners (the ones who were dragged there by Pete) were pleasantly surprised by the fresh flavors and delightful textures. Even the tea was outstanding, as well as the Chinese doughnuts. But honestly, fried balls of dough are delicious in just about any cuisine or country. It took us a while to get the hang of making quick decisions as dozens of steamer baskets were thrust in our faces, but we managed wonderfully.

↓

Cory's Approach

Cory organized her "Coolest Album Ever" into three sections. "The Travelers" section contains pictures of each of the three couples in her traveling party and their rental car. "The Adventures" section features photos and journaling of their general sightseeing. "The Laughter" section contains the silly stories and pictures of funny things that happened to them on the trip.

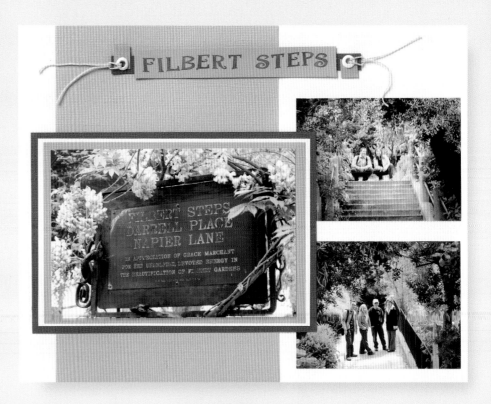

THE LAUGHING CAB DRIVER

AS RETOLD BY PETE

Luckily, there are moments in life when you can pinpoint a particular instant in time, a specific decision that leads to an experience you know you will never forget. Some of these moments involve meeting the love of your life. On this night, however, it was the choice to get in a certain taxicab. A reconstructed transcript of that cab ride follows:

LYNNE: So is this the most wonderful weather you've had here or what?!

LAUGHING CAB DRIVER: Are you kidding? Last week we had a heat wave. Everyone was complaining about how hot it was. But that's how it is in this town—everyone a whiner. "Oh, it too hot, it too cold"—when it hot they want it to be cold, when it cold, they go complain to they doctor, "it too cold, I'm sick." HAHAHAHAHAHAHA! Other day a woman whine to me, "it too cold, can I get a napkin?" HAHAHAHAHAHAHA! That how everyone is—a whiner. It never get really cold here, not like New York, or, or, or, or—

US: Boston?

Much of the delight of Cory's album is in the journaling and the journaling approach. Amusing descriptions of the San Francisco trip have been made into half-page pieces of "background paper" with a small pull tag attached. This "paper" is housed in transparent sleeves made of page protectors and sewn to the page. The photos are then positioned over the background paper. The overall design is elegant and uncluttered, and journaling can be pulled out of the sleeve by its decorative tab.

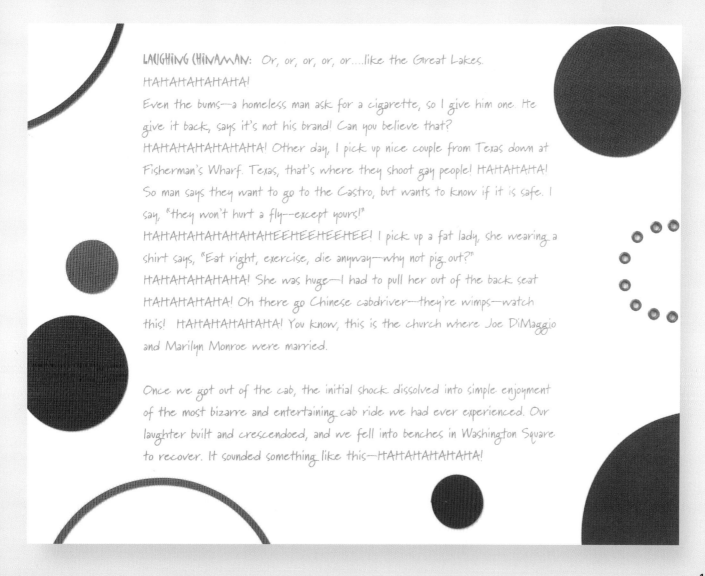

LAUGHING CHINAMAN: Or, or, or, or, or....like the Great Lakes. HAHAHAHAHAHA!

Even the bums—a homeless man ask for a cigarette, so I give him one. He give it back, says it's not his brand! Can you believe that? HAHAHAHAHAHAHA! Other day, I pick up nice couple from Texas down at Fisherman's Wharf. Texas, that's where they shoot gay people! HAHAHAHA! So man says they want to go to the Castro, but wants to know if it is safe. I say, "they won't hurt a fly—except yours!" HAHAHAHAHAHAHAHAHEEHEEHEEHEE! I pick up a fat lady, she wearing a shirt says, "Eat right, exercise, die anyway—why not pig out?" HAHAHAHAHAHA! She was huge—I had to pull her out of the back seat HAHAHAHAHA! Oh there go Chinese cabdriver—they're wimps—watch this! HAHAHAHAHAHA! You know, this is the church where Joe DiMaggio and Marilyn Monroe were married.

Once we got out of the cab, the initial shock dissolved into simple enjoyment of the most bizarre and entertaining cab ride we had ever experienced. Our laughter built and crescendoed, and we fell into benches in Washington Square to recover. It sounded something like this—HAHAHAHAHAHA!

Journaling: Tuesday: We awakened with anticipation—today we would see the Pacific Coast. But first, breakfast at Mama's. Yummy, yummy French toast on a variety of breads, and decadent omelets. We watched the locals in Washington Square Park do Tai Chi in the morning sunlight. Then, once again, we piled into that blasted Pacifica and headed north. First stop— Golden Gate Bridge. Initially, just for the bathrooms, but the bridge beckoned so we went for a stroll. We passed the first huge tower and realized we were not yet over the water, so we ventured farther, basking in the sunlight and marveling at the brilliant colors—blue water, green hills, red-orange bridge. The wind blew, as always. Onward then to Muir Woods, home of a thousand tourists and thousand-year-old Redwoods. After driving along narrow hillside roads which appeared deceptively untraveled, we parked in the overflow lot and strolled into the woods. (Sky: brilliant blue. Temperature: perfect in the sun, just cool enough in the shade to appreciate the sun.) Well, there were lots of people, but the trees towered over us and reminded us of our briefness, in the scope of things. These trees were somber and stately, serious among the laughing children and unending photographs. We took our share of pictures and moved onward toward the coast. A view of the ocean was next. From our perch on Muir Beach, we could see back to San Francisco, north along the coast, and out across the Pacific. It was chilly and blustery, but quite a sight to take in. We made our way to Stitson Beach for a picnic lunch and search for soda. There were many people out on the beach, some getting wet, but none swimming. Another drive took us to part of the Matt Davis Trail at Pan Toll. A one and a half mile hike through forest brought us out into a hillside overlooking the ocean. Lounging, stretching, deer watching, a jog up a hill (Pete), and general staring in wonder were the activities of choice.

GOLDEN GATE bridge

Before you leave home, consider these tips to make later scrapbooking of your journey an easier and more meaningful project.

Before Your Vacation

Note the places that family and friends are most excited about seeing. Plan to use key words as prompts. When anyone says anything is "cool" or "beautiful," it's your cue to get the camera or notebook out.

Pack a binder with page protectors in it to organize maps, ticket stubs, brochures, postcards, restaurant and hotel receipt and other travel memorabilia that you'll collect.

Pack a diary or travel journal. Plan to jot down place names and the highlights of each day. You'll be amazed what you remember later from a line or two written then and there.

During Your Vacation

Take at least a few photos of each traveler. Many scrapbooks get put on hold because there is not a single picture of one family member or friend.

Note or photograph the places where you eat, the food you order and its cost.

Buy two sets of identical postcards. Write on one. Mail one to yourself. Display them side-by-side in your vacation album—one face up and the mailed one face down. Your journaling will be done and dated, and you will have a postage stamp "embellishment" on your page.

Look for signage opportunities and use them. Town or National Park signs, historic markers, road signs or hiking trail signposts are all good ways to "title" pages or to provide additional journaling.

After Your Vacation

When your traveling companions are around, pull out photos, videos and memorabilia and jot down what they remember most.

Organize your journey scrapbook in the most logical way for your trip: by location; by sight, sound and taste; by land and sea; by the adventurers and the adventure; by the things that went as planned and the things that did not; by day one, day two and so on; or by each traveler's favorite destination.

Whether your travels are close to home or world wide, a journey album will allow you to revisit and share your travels whenever its pages are opened.

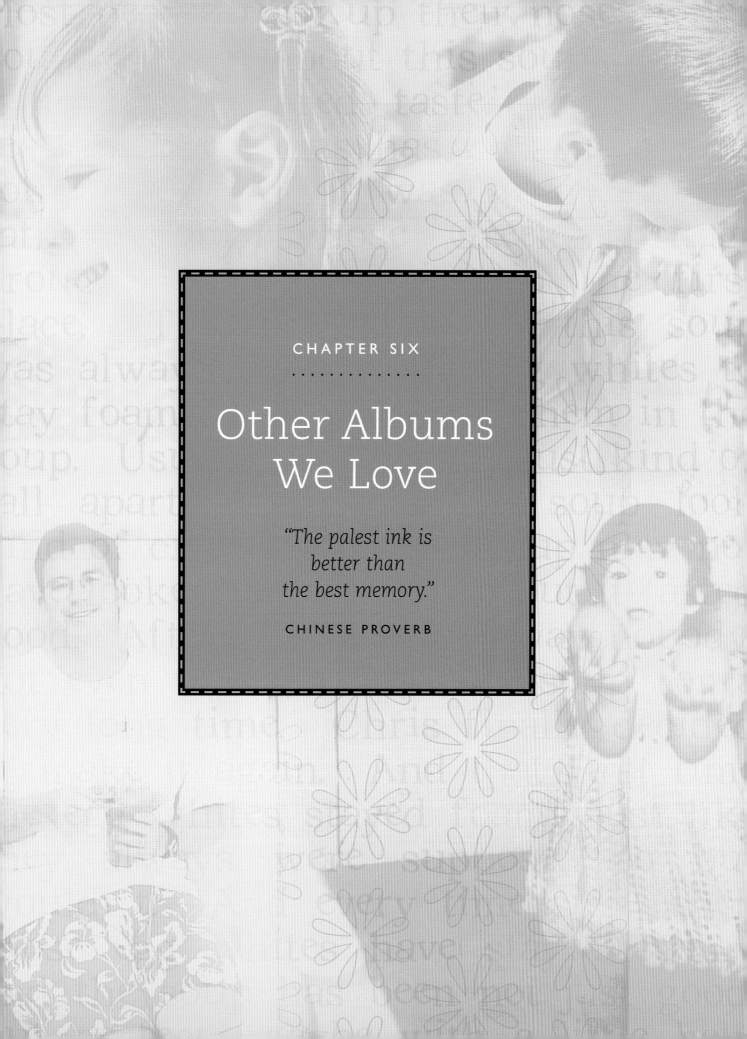

CHAPTER SIX

· · · · · · · · · · · · ·

Other Albums
We Love

*"The palest ink is
better than
the best memory."*

CHINESE PROVERB

Our "Coolest Album Ever" contest was one of the hardest that the Simple Scrapbooks staff ever had to judge. After the winners had been selected, we were still left with another large stack of heartwarming albums that we really loved. Here are just a few of those "other" albums.

Hawaii is a holiday destination anyone would relish, but **Amy Trask's** trip was much more than a vacation. Her husband had been raised in the Islands. Amy's album documents her chance to experience his precious family memories.

Julie Dominguez' album was carefully crafted as a gift for her soon-to-be three-year-old daughter. It is full of the friends, family, food and fun in her daughter's third year of life.

Food, family and fun are also part of **Samantha VanArnhem's** legacy album. This delightful scrapbook is a cookbook and family history combination that celebrates Samantha's Greek and Italian heritage.

Words were hard to come by for **Sarah Little** until she found a clever way to tell her husband how she felt about his relationship with their son.

Tish Treadaway believed most of her family memorabilia had been destroyed in a heart-wrenching house fire in 1978. Her self-discovery album is made richer for photos she believed were long gone.

Some albums document a life, a year, a vacation, or a special day. **Sherri Horton's** tiny album captures one small and simple moment in spring.

These albums range from immense volumes that cover an entire life span, to the tiniest of treasures that capture a few small moments in time. They represent the many other albums that didn't find a place in this book, but truly found a place in our hearts. Enjoy!

Dear Mom and Dad,
Thank you so much for having us with you in Hawaii. We hope this album reminds you of the sights, sounds, and tastes of our wonderful trip together.
—Carl and Amy

Amy tells us that Hawaiians put beans in the bottom of their snow cones.

Amy made her "Coolest Album Ever" as a gift for her in-laws. It was a "thank you" for a priceless journey Amy, her husband and her in-laws took together in July 2004. Amy's husband Carl was born in Hawaii and lived there off and on during his childhood. But Amy had never been to the islands, so her in-laws took her to all the places that were special to her husband's

childhood. They also made a point to treat her to the tastes of her husband's growing-up years.

They went to Zippy's, the family's favorite fast food restaurant where Carl used to eat as a child, and to Leonard's, the family's preferred "malasadas" (donut) shop. They also stopped in at Matsumoto's for shaved-ice, popular with locals and tourists alike. They drove by the houses where the family had lived and the hospital where Carl was born. Amy's gift album was made in a spirit of deepest gratitude and is a reflection of all the relived sights, sounds, and tastes of the family's years in Hawaii.

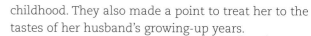

Amy's Approach

Amy's scrapbooking approach to her very special Hawaiian holiday is an unusual but practical one. She divides her album into Sights, Sounds and Tastes. While the sights and music of different cultures are often celebrated, using "Tastes" as one of her organizing principles gave Amy a place to showcase the restaurants of her husband's childhood.

SHAVE ICE

M. MATSUMOTO GROCERY STORE

I could tell by the line stretching out the door at Matsumoto's that I was in for no ordinary snow cone. Beans, soft-serve, and packed ice, cut straight from a block combined make the best shaved ice on the island (or so one "native" Hawaiian tells me).

Whoever invented that drip catcher is a *genius*. The best 25¢ ever spent!

- flavored syrup
- shave ice
- azuki beans
- ice cream

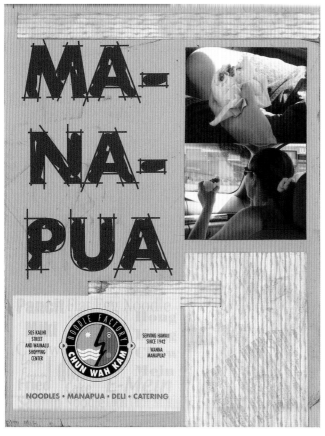

MA-
NA-
PUA

505 KALIHI STREET AND WAIMALU SHOPPING CENTER

CHUN WAH KAM
NOODLE FACTORY

SERVING HAWAII SINCE 1942 WANNA MANAPUA?

NOODLES • MANAPUA • DELI • CATERING

HOT malasadas

Leonard's

MALASADAS
PÃO-DÔCE

Dear Anna,

You are turning three years old in just a few weeks. This has been an amazing year in which you have changed from a docile toddler to a highly opinionated little girl. You are very funny and make us laugh every day. Some of the things you say keep us laughing for days or even weeks afterwards. Every time I think you are at the absolute cutest stage possible, you prove me wrong by getting even cuter and sweeter. When we tell you how cute you are,

"I'm not cute, I'm two!"

you say, "I'm not cute, I'm two!" I decided on a whim that I needed to try to capture some of the funny things you have said or done. That list of funny quotes evolved into this scrapbook. Compiling these stories and pictures brought back many happy memories for Daddy and me. A few weeks ago you started telling me that I am your very best friend and that you love me too much. I love you too and I hope we will always have these kinds of fun times together.

Love,

Mommy

As a two-year-old, Anna Dominguez "needed" 21 toys and books in her bed to get to sleep at night.

This album is a celebration of the year Julie's daughter Anna was two years old. It captures many of the cute things Anna said and did as well as the some of the milestones of the year. When it was finished it became one of Anna's most prized possessions and she cried when she realized it was being sent away to be photographed.

Julie's Approach

When Julie decided to make an album for Anna's birthday, she looked through the year's pictures to see which ones she wanted to include. She wanted as many little snippets of her daughter's personality, life and friends as possible. Julie especially wanted to include photos that were not strong enough individually to be the focus of a regular scrapbook page. By using them with other pictures, quotes and journaling, she was able to include them and make a more complete album. The photos and facts of Anna's young life were easily categorized into Fun, Food, Family, Friends and Festivities, so Julie used these as sections to organize her album.

Julie's album is all digital. She created it in Adobe PhotoShop Elements. Embossing and drop shadows give all of the buttons and photos visual depth. Tags hold little journaling lists. The pictures are very random, so she stuck with a simple layout and color scheme.

The album does not contain three-dimensional embellishments, so it's not particularly fragile; Julie is quite comfortable letting Anna play with it unsupervised. And since each page is simply a digital image, it can easily be reprinted if it becomes too worn or damaged.

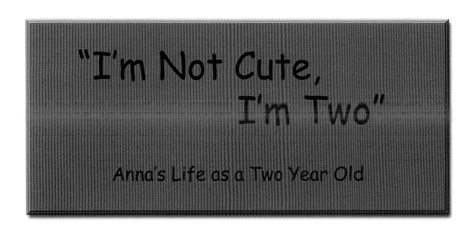

Food

You spend many hours pretending to prepare and serve up everything from cherry pie to iced coffee to anyone, or any doll, that will accept your offer. This summer you started making a lot of pretend lattés with "lotfat milk". One day I gave you a taste of an unsweetened latté and you found it to be so gross that you spit it back into the cup. I haven't heard much about lattés since that day. Two more things you probably regret trying are Lily's rice cereal and her bottle of formula. They clearly weren't the wonderful treat you had been expecting.

You love to help Daddy and me make pancakes, cookies and muffins. Sometimes you help make dinner by slicing olives with an egg slicer or tearing bread for casseroles. You love to pour ingredients into the bread machine and it probably won't be long until you can make your own loaf of bread! You can make bean burritos with a fair amount of independence. You also like to spread peanut butter and jelly or cream cheese, which seems to be more about licking the knife than the actual spreading!

You are aware of your food allergies and always ask whether or not new foods contain corn syrup. You have been "reading the gedients" on food packages since before you turned two and continue to do so periodically. This summer you came running from your bedroom into the kitchen, screaming in anguish. You were making a pretend cake and accidentally put corn syrup in it. I asked if it had made you sick and you said no, that you couldn't even eat it.

Favorite Snacks & Treats
frozen peas
baby carrots
cereal bars
pretzels
fruit
chips
Krispy Kreme doughnuts
muffins

Favorite Lunches & Breakfasts
bean burrito
Annie's mac & cheese
hot dog
cheese & crackers
bagel
toast with pb&j
cereal with milk
waffles
pancakes

Favorite Dinners & Desserts
pizza
chili
cheeseburger
steak
beans & rice
tacos
scalloped potatoes
ice cream
homemade cookies

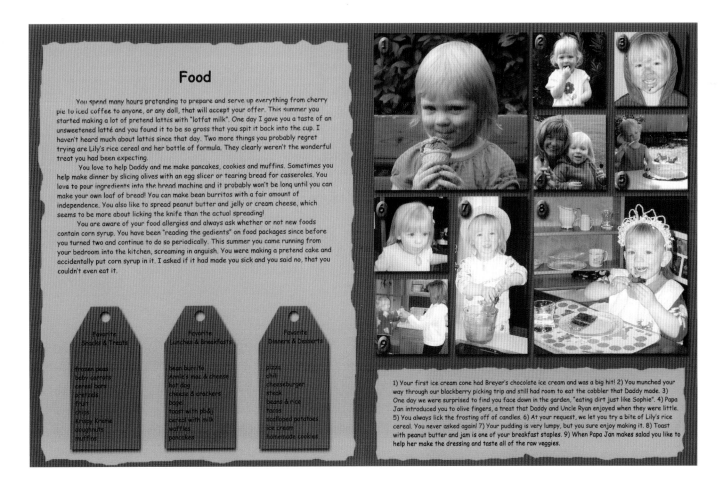

1) Your first ice cream cone had Breyer's chocolate ice cream and was a big hit! 2) You munched your way through our blackberry picking trip and still had room to eat the cobbler that Daddy made. 3) One day we were surprised to find you face down in the garden, "eating dirt just like Sophie". 4) Papa Jan introduced you to olive fingers, a treat that Daddy and Uncle Ryan enjoyed when they were little. 5) You always lick the frosting off of candles. 6) At your request, we let you try a bite of Lily's rice cereal. You never asked again! 7) Your pudding is very lumpy, but you sure enjoy making it. 8) Toast with peanut butter and jam is one of your breakfast staples. 9) When Papa Jan makes salad you like to help her make the dressing and taste all of the raw veggies.

Journaling: You spend many hours pretending to prepare and serve up everything from cherry pie to iced coffee to anyone, or any doll, that will accept your offer. This summer you started making a lot of pretend lattes with "lotfat milk." One day I gave you a taste of an unsweetened latte and you found it to be so gross that you spit it back into the cup. I haven't heard much about lattes since that day. Two more things you probably regret trying are Lily's rice cereal and her bottle of formula. They clearly weren't the wonderful treat you had been expecting.

You love to help Dad and me make pancakes, cookies and muffins. Sometimes you help make dinner by slicing olives with an egg slicer or tearing bread for casseroles. You love to pour ingredients into the bread machine and it probably won't be long until you can make your own loaf of bread. You can make bean burritos with a fair amount of independence. You also like to spread peanut butter and jelly or cream cheese, which seems to be more about licking the knife than actual spreading.

You are aware of your food allergies and always ask whether or not new foods contain corn syrup. You have been "reading the gedients" on food packages since before you turned two and continue to do so periodically. This summer you came running from your bedroom into the kitchen, screaming in anguish. You were making a pretend cake and accidentally put corn syrup in it. I asked if it had made you sick and you said no, that you couldn't even eat it.

Favorite Snacks & Treats
- frozen peas
- baby carrots
- cereal bars
- pretzels
- fruit
- chips
- Krispy Kreme doughnuts
- muffins

Favorite Lunches & Breakfasts
- bean burrito
- Annie's mac & cheese
- hot dog
- cheese & crackers
- bagel
- toast with pb&j
- cereal with milk
- waffles
- pancakes

Favorite Dinners & Desserts
- pizza
- chili
- cheeseburger
- steak
- beans & rice
- tacos
- scalloped potatoes
- ice cream
- homemade cookies

"Having an Italian and Greek heritage makes food an important part of what brings our family together. There are so many dishes that are unique to us and could never be found in any cookbook exactly the way we make them. I was concerned about these important pieces of our family history not being fully documented somewhere, and that the recipes and stories about them could someday be lost. So I created this book not only as a tribute to the recipes, but to the people who create them each time with love and care."

Our Family Favorites

made with love

This book contains a collection of the favorite recipes of three generations of our family. Each recipe is accompanied by the story of where it originated from and what makes it such a special part of our family history. Unlike traditional cookbooks, each chapter of this book is dedicated to a cook. We are grandmothers, mothers, sisters, daughters or aunts - each of us has our own cooking style very different from one another.

This book also contains fun little tidbits about each of us to give you some idea of what kind of cooks we are and just maybe what kind of women we are too.

cooking done with care is an act of love

created in 2004 by Samantha VanArnhem

RECIPES

The secret ingredient in Samantha's family's spaghetti sauce is Mantey Vineyards' Old Fashioned Blue Face Concord Wine.

A family cookbook, complete with photos of the cooks and stories of the family, is a wonderful way to showcase your heritage and family traditions. What better way to capture the flavor of a family than to journal about the food they eat?

Samantha's mixed Greek and Italian heritage was a wonderful blend of culture and food that she wanted to be sure was documented. In her album "Our Family Favorites," Samantha scrapbooks the heritage recipes, the personalities, the traditions and even the cooking disasters.

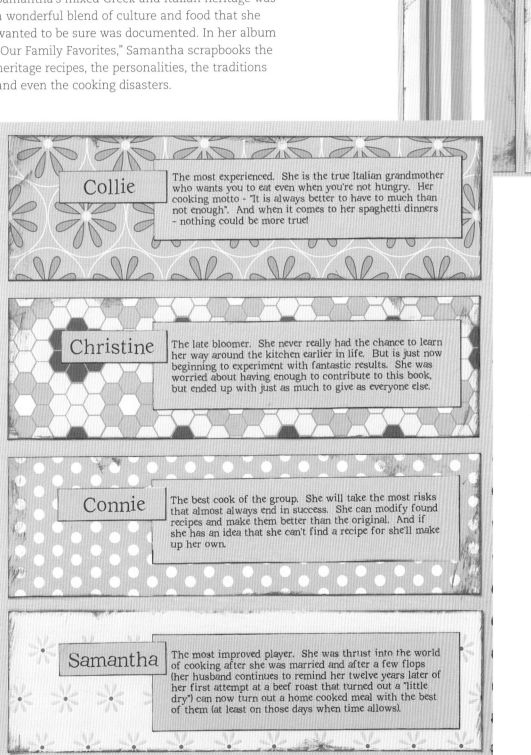

Samantha

Collie
The most experienced. She is the true Italian grandmother who wants you to eat even when you're not hungry. Her cooking motto - "It is always better to have to much than not enough". And when it comes to her spaghetti dinners - nothing could be more true!

Christine
The late bloomer. She never really had the chance to learn her way around the kitchen earlier in life. But is just now beginning to experiment with fantastic results. She was worried about having enough to contribute to this book, but ended up with just as much to give as everyone else.

Connie
The best cook of the group. She will take the most risks that almost always end in success. She can modify found recipes and make them better than the original. And if she has an idea that she can't find a recipe for she'll make up her own.

Samantha
The most improved player. She was thrust into the world of cooking after she was married and after a few flops (her husband continues to remind her twelve years later of her first attempt at a beef roast that turned out a "little dry") can now turn out a home cooked meal with the best of them (at least on those days when time allows).

Spaghetti Sauce

1 small yellow onion   Parsley
2-3 cloves fresh garlic   Oregano
1 jar Ragu traditional sauce   Basil
1 8oz can of tomato sauce   Garlic Powder
Parmesan Cheese   Pepper
Gram-pa Mantey's Concord Wine

Finely chop onion and garlic. In a large saucepan saute onion and
garlic in vegetable oil. Add jar of Ragu. Fill the empty jar 1-2
inches with water and add to sauce. Add tomato sauce plus one
can of water. Season with remaining ingredients to taste. Simmer
over medium heat for at least 30 minutes. Continue to simmer
over low heat for an additional 30 minutes.

This is THE sauce. We all
grew up eating this sauce and
nothing else will ever match
it. Most sauces are too sweet
in comparison. Of course
there are no formal measurements for the seasonings.
Grammie has perfected those
measurements by sight not a
measuring spoon. The secret
ingredient is Grampa Mantey's
Old Fashioned Blue Face
Concord Wine, which is
produced by Mantey Vine-
yards in Sandusky, Ohio. It
may not be a fancy wine but
it adds a taste to this sauce
that makes it uniquely
Grammie's.

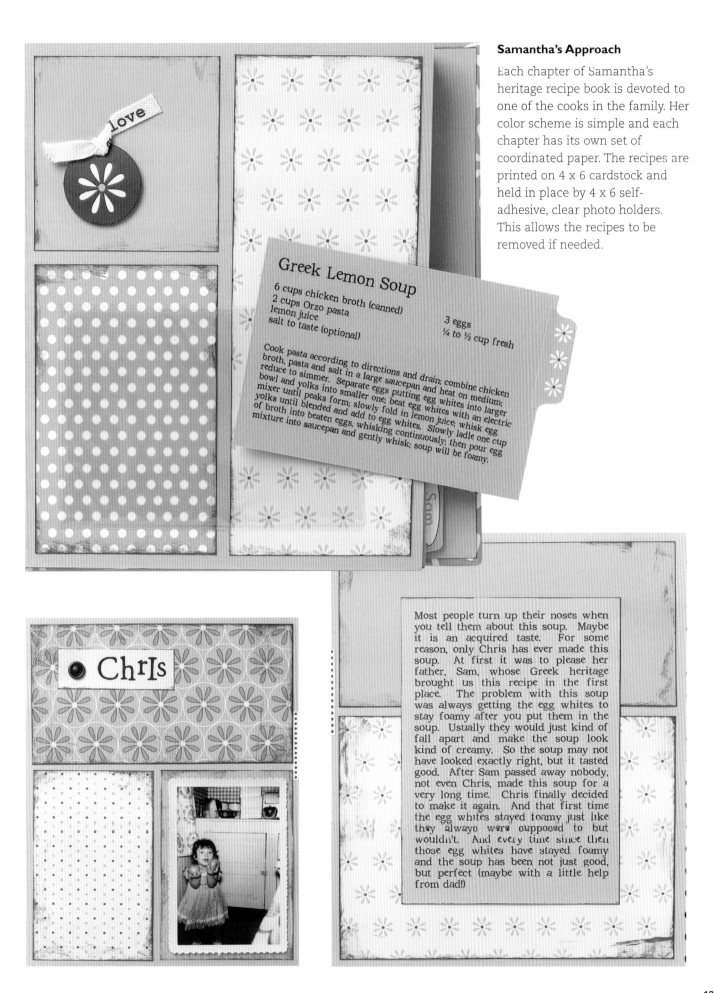

Samantha's Approach

Each chapter of Samantha's heritage recipe book is devoted to one of the cooks in the family. Her color scheme is simple and each chapter has its own set of coordinated paper. The recipes are printed on 4 x 6 cardstock and held in place by 4 x 6 self-adhesive, clear photo holders. This allows the recipes to be removed if needed.

Greek Lemon Soup

6 cups chicken broth (canned)
2 cups Orzo pasta
lemon juice
salt to taste (optional)

3 eggs
¼ to ½ cup fresh

Cook pasta according to directions and drain; combine chicken broth, pasta and salt in a large saucepan and heat on medium; reduce to simmer. Separate eggs putting egg whites into larger bowl and yolks into smaller one; beat egg whites with an electric mixer until peaks form; slowly fold in lemon juice; whisk egg yolks until blended and add to egg whites. Slowly ladle one cup of broth into beaten eggs, whisking continuously; then pour egg mixture into saucepan and gently whisk; soup will be foamy.

Chris

Most people turn up their noses when you tell them about this soup. Maybe it is an acquired taste. For some reason, only Chris has ever made this soup. At first it was to please her father, Sam, whose Greek heritage brought us this recipe in the first place. The problem with this soup was always getting the egg whites to stay foamy after you put them in the soup. Usually they would just kind of fall apart and make the soup look kind of creamy. So the soup may not have looked exactly right, but it tasted good. After Sam passed away nobody, not even Chris, made this soup for a very long time. Chris finally decided to make it again. And that first time the egg whites stayed foamy just like they always were supposed to but wouldn't. And every time since then those egg whites have stayed foamy and the soup has been not just good, but perfect (maybe with a little help from dad!)

"Todd, Xander has so much to learn from you. What a wonderful man he will grow to be—what a great father he will become—what a life he will lead—all because he has you for his father."

Xander isn't a year old yet, but his Dad already knows how important he is in Xander's life.

Sarah's husband was so excited to be a dad. For his first Father's Day she wanted to make an album highlighting all the reasons why his relationship with their son is so important. She struggled to find the right words for her album, until she found the book *Why a Son Needs a Dad*, by Greg E. Lang. Phrases taken from Long's book said everything Sarah wanted to say. Even though the words were not all her own, there were several times when she was assembling the album that she had to pause and wait for the tears to stop. Her hopes and dreams for the relationship between her husband and their son shine through in her thoughtful gift.

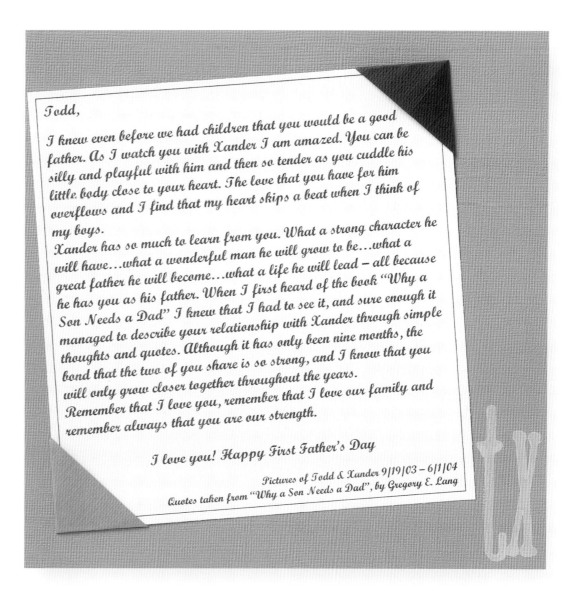

Todd,

I knew even before we had children that you would be a good father. As I watch you with Xander I am amazed. You can be silly and playful with him and then so tender as you cuddle his little body close to your heart. The love that you have for him overflows and I find that my heart skips a beat when I think of my boys.

Xander has so much to learn from you. What a strong character he will have…what a wonderful man he will grow to be…what a great father he will become…what a life he will lead – all because he has you as his father. When I first heard of the book "Why a Son Needs a Dad" I knew that I had to see it, and sure enough it managed to describe your relationship with Xander through simple thoughts and quotes. Although it has only been nine months, the bond that the two of you share is so strong, and I know that you will only grow closer together throughout the years. Remember that I love you, remember that I love our family and remember always that you are our strength.

I love you! Happy First Father's Day

Pictures of Todd & Xander 9/19/03 – 6/1/04
Quotes taken from "Why a Son Needs a Dad", by Gregory E. Lang

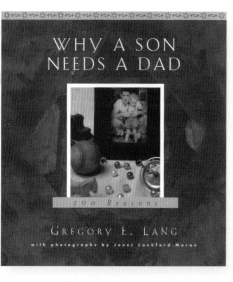

WHY A SON
NEEDS A DAD

100 Reasons

GREGORY E. LANG
with photographs by Janet Lankford-Moran

a son needs a dad…

Who has experienced the joys in life
and wants to share those moments with his son.

Who lives with integrity-
a man with standards, principles and good character.

Who has grown from boy to man
and will take that journey again with his son.

Who holds his responsibilities as a husband and a father
as his highest priority.

To take him to baseball games.

Who is willing to make sacrifices for his family.

To teach him how to be a gentleman.

To teach him to be respectful of women.

To teach him that men and women are equals.

So that he will have at least one hero he can depend on.

Sarah's Approach

Sarah found the right words for her album in a book about fathers and sons. Inspiration for your journaling is all around you. Put your subject matter in a search engine on the Internet and see what comes up. Go to the electronic card catalog at your library. Look through old letters or school papers. Ask friends and family for ideas. Sit down and just start writing. The story really is the scrapbook, so think through this important part of making your coolest album.

| SPECIAL MENTION | Tish Treadaway \| HARRISBURG, NC | Celebrate my Life |

"I am excited to present Simple Scrapbooks with my version of an all-about-me album. A special note of appreciation to Creating Keepsakes magazine for the inspiration and motivation to encourage me to complete my 'Coolest Album.'"

A family fire had left Tish Treadaway with little hope of finding childhood memorabilia she could use to make her own self-discovery album.

"Celebrate my Life" is a true album of self discovery. In January 2003, Tish was inspired by a magazine article to create a theme album about herself. Since she is usually the person behind the camera, she decided to change her focus. The article had suggested completing a page a month, and that sounded simple enough!

Tish returned to her hometown in east Texas to gather information and snap photos of childhood landmarks to help her prepare for the project. She was not expecting to find too much to mark her childhood. She believed most of the family memorabilia had been destroyed in a heart-wrenching house fire in 1978. As she dug through numerous boxes in her parents' attic, she was surprised and elated to discover many old school photos, childhood artwork, and report cards and letters that had somehow escaped the fire.

As Tish sifted through pieces of her childhood, she began to understand more about herself and her family. She now had pieces of her story that could connect her and her children to their past. Boxes of photos and memorabilia, that would have been meaningless to her children without their mother to narrate them, are now highlighted in a gift album she hopes they'll treasure.

Just as our eyes are drawn toward's life's beauty... our thoughts linger on those who have touched our hearts.

Virgilio Vicco Gonzalez
May 4, 1923

This special man is the first love of my life. He continues to touch my heart and actively participate in my life. He has loved me unconditionally and been there to supported me through the low valley's and cheered me on while on mountain tops in my life. He has been a very supportive father, friend, mentor and grandfather to my three children. He is the most generous person that I have ever know. His zest for life and positive attitude can be seen and felt by all that have met him. I hope and pray that I can pass his passion for life on to my children. I love, respect and cherish you with all my heart! Thank you for providing a safe, secure and wonderful life for my family!

Celebrate my Life

- Leticia Anne Gonzalez Treadaway
- Born - April 19, 1960
  Birthplace - Dallas, Texas
- I am five foot, four inches tall, olive color skin, dark brown hair and brown eyes.
- I am the fifth child out of six children, the baby girl!
- My mother was born in Big Springs, Texas, on August 8, 1929 and died June 30, 1999.
- My father is a native Filipino born in San Raffael, Philippines on May 4, 1923.
- Married Tony Treadaway February 1, 1999

My mother is an individual who encouraged me to be strong. Not to sell myself short and that I had the strength to do anything. She seemed to be an individual that had no fear. She gained her strength from her faith in the Lord. I would often come across her while she was in quiet meditation. My mother loved her role as a wife and mother of six children. She was loving, caring and nurturing. I miss our late night phone calls, her news updates on world events and sharing the kids accomplishments. I miss the fact that she isn't here to see my kids grow up to be fine young men and young lady. I only hope they have enough memories of her in their hearts to impact their lives.

Mary Louise Long- Gonzalez
August 8, 1929-June 30, 1999

Treasures

The handing down of knowledge
From generations unsurpassed,
Beliefs and customs taught,
Strongly rooted in our past.

Linking our tomorrows with
The treasures of yesterday,
A precious gift that can be cherished
And shared along the way.
— Brenda Darlene Kijowski

The brass pieces came from
family, the small one belonged
to Tony's mother, the tall one
belonged to my mother

Growing up...
I was embarrassed to have a father that was Fillipino because
neighborhood kids harrassed me for being different. Now I
am proud of my heritage and the journey my father made
to the United States to seek a future here!

I am a hopeless romantic!

I was a little sister in
my brother's fraternity.

I'm a
Daddy's
Girl

I played basketball when girls
played half-court with 6 players.

I received my first "scrapbook" when I was 12
Years old, a golden color burlap book. I
participated in the Yearbook staff in highschool.
Now I am a shutter bug and a scrapbook fanatic.

Drinking age was 18 Years old. I made a huge blunder
one night by taking my underage little brother out for a
drink. I didn't realize that he had a few too many,
well...I was grounded for what seemed like an eternity.

MY first boyfriend was Keith Holy, we met in
Kindergarten. In first grade, he gave me my "first
kiss" the teacher, a Catholic Nun was not very excited
about the incident. She took this opportunity to teach
our class on the hazzards of kissing and passing germs!

Sharing Secrets

138

Tish's Approach

Tish uses a variety of interesting topics to help her organize her self-discovery album. Among our favorites are "My Daily Routine" and "Treasures." On her "Daily Routine" page, Tish organizes her day into three sections. One deals with her morning routine, another with her midday activities and a third with a typical evening schedule.

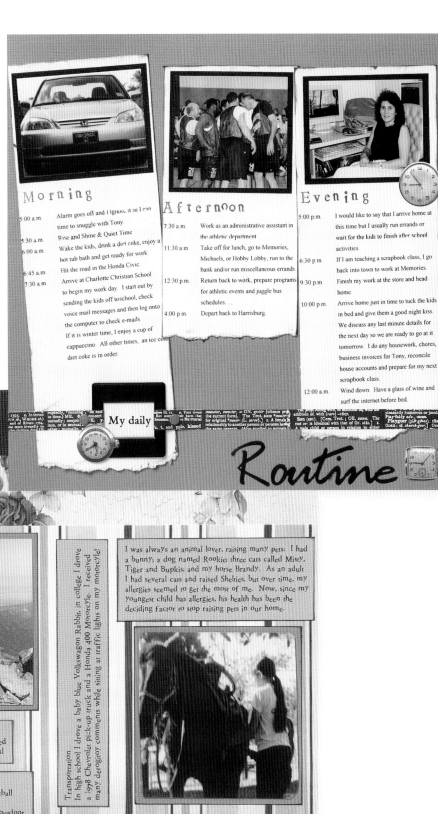

Morning

5:00 a.m.　Alarm goes off and I ignore it so I can time to snuggle with Tony.

5:30 a.m.　Rise and Shine & Quiet Time

6:00 a.m.　Wake the kids, drink a diet coke, enjoy a hot tub bath and get ready for work.

6:45 a.m.　Hit the road in the Honda Civic.

7:30 a.m.　Arrive at Charlotte Christian School to begin my work day. I start out by sending the kids off to school, check voice mail messages and then log onto the computer to check e-mails.
If it is winter time, I enjoy a cup of cappuccino. All other times, an ice cold diet coke is in order.

Afternoon

7:30 a.m.　Work as an administrative assistant in the athletic department

11:30 a.m.　Take off for lunch, go to Memories, Michaels, or Hobby Lobby, run to the bank and/or run miscellaneous errands.

12:30 p.m.　Return back to work, prepare programs for athletic events and juggle bus schedules.....

4:00 p.m.　Depart back to Harrisburg.

Evening

5:00 p.m.　I would like to say that I arrive home at this time but I usually run errands or wait for the kids to finish after school activities.

6:30 p.m.　If I am teaching a scrapbook class, I go back into town to work at Memories.

9:30 p.m.　Finish my work at the store and head home.

10:00 p.m.　Arrive home just in time to tuck the kids in bed and give them a good night kiss. We discuss any last minute details for the next day so we are ready to go at it tomorrow. I do any housework, chores, business invoices for Tony, reconcile house accounts and prepare for my next scrapbook class.

12:00 a.m.　Wind down. Have a glass of wine and surf the internet before bed.

My daily

Routine

I was always an animal lover, raising many pets: I had a bunny, a dog named Rookie, three cats called Misty, Tiger and Bupkis, and my horse Brandy. As an adult I had several cats and raised Shelties, but over time, my allergies seemed to get the most of me. Now, since my youngest child has allergies, his health has been the deciding factor to stop raising pets in our home.

Growing up I was a tomboy; I hung around with my brothers and their friends. My favorite clothes included blue jeans, t-shirt, hiking boots and an army jacket, and

Life's humor...
In high school I was a jock running track, playing basketball and even took Tae Kwon Do Karate. In college I was a member of the Texas Tech Outdoor Club that went on outdoor excursions to New Mexico and Colorado. My longest hiking trip in the mountains was a week. I feel like I did a full circle in my life. I now work in the athletic department in a school,

Transportation:
In high school I drove a baby blue Volkswagon Rabbit, in college I drove a 1978 Chevrolet pick-up truck and a Honda 400 Motorcyle. I received many derogitoy comments while sitting at traffic lights on my motorcyle!

from the Past...

My Spiritual Journey...

I was born into a devout Catholic family and attended private Catholic schools to reinforce my faith. Having teachers that were nuns dressed in habits, taking religion classes throughout my early years and attending mass with my family was the extent of my faith. I was never really exposed to other religious denominations until I attended college at Texas Tech University. While in college I put my religious beliefs aside believing I was saved by my birth as a Catholic.

After graduation from college, I married into a family that attended a variety of churches and

exposure that challenged me to read the Bible for

Church. Steve and Joni were very kind and invited us to attend their church. It was this

"This album is my celebration of spring. The beginning of spring brings a celebration of newness when our days get longer and new things begin to blossom and grow around us."

I love spring anywhere,
But if I could choose
I would always greet it
in the garden.

Ruth Stout

Spring comes to the Horton house in small bursts of color and curiosity.

In her delightful little album "March," Sherri Horton shows us a celebration not just of spring, but also of family. Her album shows her boys outside, checking on the progress of spring.

beginnings

PLEASURES

142

Sherri's Approach

The light blue cardstock used in Sherri's album matches her boy's sweaters and is the perfect background for spring blossoms and budding childhood. Intriguing photos pull us in to this mini album. We want to know what the children are looking at, what have they've discovered. Curiosity about freshly blooming life becomes contagious. Sherri's photography and design style enable her to pack a lot of feeling in one very tiny package.

Materials Index

CHAPTER ONE—TRIBUTES

Within These Walls
Beth Proudfoot | Clinton, NJ

album 6 × 6 mini book, kraft cover with envelope (Making Memories)
stickers (Making Memories)
foam stamps (Making Memories)
pewter brads (Making Memories)
ribbon (Making Memories and Offray)
button (Hillcreek Designs)
tags (DMD Industries, Inc.)
font Geneva

In Our Own Words
Angie R. Hunt | Greensboro, GA

album 6 × 6 Outdoor Denim (Close To My Heart)
patterned paper (Rusty Pickle, 7gypsies, Close To My Heart and PSX)
stamps (Close To My Heart)
eyelets (Close To My Heart)
photo corners (Close To My Heart)
fonts Goudy Old Style, CK Cursive, Century Schoolbook, Times New Roman, ITC Kristen, ITC Viner Hand, American Classic, Needlepoint, Engravers MT, Monotype Corsiva, CK Nifty, First Grader and Rockwell

Case File Confidential
Lori Robb | Lehi, UT

album 4½ × 6¾ handcrafted by Lori, based entirely on EK Success Clue paper
patterned paper (EK Success, Nostalgia, Paperbilities, Provo Craft and K&Company)
stickers footprints (EK Success)
eyelets (Making Memories)
stamping ink (Tsukineko)
font Mom's Typewriter

Once Upon a Quilt
Lisa Moorefield | Burlington, NC

album 14 × 14 quilt handcrafted by Lisa using fabric scraps, folded and pinned to 6 × 12 page protectors with quilt basting pins
ribbon (Offray)
fonts 39 Smooth and Hootie

CHAPTER TWO—CELEBRATIONS

A Prom Night to Remember
Nancy Kreider | New Providence, PA

album 8 × 8 (Colorbök)
patterned paper (Robin's Nest Designs)
stickers (Creative Imaginations)
photo corners (3L, Corp.)
fonts Prom Invitation, CK Cursive and Lucida Casual

McLennan Family Reunion
Nancy Nally | Palm Coast, FL

album 8 × 8 (Pulp Paper Products)
patterned paper (Making Memories and EK Success)
stickers alphabet (Making Memories)
brads (Making Memories)
metal embellishments (Making Memories and K&Company)
paper roses (Creative Elements)
font CK Cosmopolitan
acknowledgements logo design on "Sure It's Peach" by Michael Nally, photos on "All Dressed Up" by Kathy McLennan

Robin & Ken Wedding Guest Book
Dot Keil | Columbus, OH

album 8½ × 11 (Creative Memories)
stickers metal wedding (Generations)
stamps Swirl Alphabet (All Night Media)
font Book Antiqua

CHAPTER THREE—SELF DISCOVERY

"I"
Mou Saha | Tampa, FL

album 8 1/2 × 11 (Pioneer Photo Albums, Inc.)
patterned paper (Paperbilities and The Paper Company)
stickers Shotz Wordz clear epoxy (Creative Imaginations)
stamps (All Night Media)
brads (Jo-Ann Scrap Essentials)
bookplates (Jo-Ann Scrap Essentials)
vellum tags (Jo-Ann Scrap Essentials)
metal charms (Jo-Ann Scrap Essentials)
fabric (Jo-Ann Scrap Essentials)
chalk (EK Success)
unknown embroidery floss
font Century Gothic

CHAPTER FOUR—RELATIONSHIPS

30 Reasons to Love My Life
Jennifer Adams Donnelly | Crestwood, IL

album slipcase and three 4 × 5 mini albums handcrafted by Jennifer
patterned papers (7gypsies, Anna Griffin, Inc., Amscan, Bucilla, Colorbök, Design Originals, K&Company, NRN Designs and The Paper Patch)
stickers (Colorbök, C-Thru Ruler Co., EK Success, John Grossman, K&Company, NRN Designs, Paper House Productions, Sticker Studio and Wordsworth)
stamps (All Night Media, Club Scrap, Hero Arts, Inkadinkado, Making Memories, Office Max, Postmodern Design, PSX, Rubber Stampede, Stampabilities and Stampendous)
rub-ons (Creative Imaginations, Making Memories and Wilson Jones)
eyelets (Making Memories)
fiber (Lion Brand and DMC)
skeletonized leaves (Club Scrap)
metal embellishments (Amaco, Chronicle Books, Darice, EK Success and Making Memories)
tags (Avery, Mrs. Grossman, me & my BIG ideas, Paper Bliss and Westrim)
unknown pins and ribbon
fonts Phosphorus, Kelmscott Roman and Berylium

My First 35 Miles
Marnie Flores | Madison, WI

album 8½ × 7½ handcrafted by Marnie
patterned paper (BasicGrey)
flower (Making Memories)
washer (Making Memories)
rub-ons (Making Memories)
photo holders (Making Memories)
ribbon (May Arts, Midori and Offray)
button (Hillcreek Designs)
fonts P22 Garamouche, MA Sexy and Butterbrotpapier

CHAPTER FOUR—RELATIONSHIPS

Mom and Me
Sarah Doyle | Rockford, IL

album 6 × 6 (We R Memory Keepers)
patterned paper (Magenta)
stickers (Li'l Davis Designs)
stamps (Making Memories)
safety pins (Making Memories)
rub-ons (Making Memories, Li'l Davis Designs and Junkitz)
fonts Two Peas Stained Glass

My Precious Friend, Baby
Kendra Wietstock | Goshen, IN

album 8 × 8 (Mrs. Grossman's)
metal frames (Making Memories)
silver word charms (Colorbök)
black bubble phrases (Li'l Davis Designs)
pewter holders (Li'l Davis Designs)

Dad, What I Learned
JoAnne Hoatson | North Platte, NE

album Perfect Fit 6 × 6 (Making Memories)
patterned paper (Carolee's Creations, 7gypsies, Creative Imaginations, American Crafts, Francis Meyer, K&Company, SEI, KI Memories, Chatterbox, Inc., and Anna Griffin, Inc.)
stamps (Making Memories)
brads (Making Memories and Eyelets, Etc.)
eyelets (Making Memories and Eyelets, Etc.)
tags (Making Memories)
safety pins (Making Memories)
conchos (Scrapworks)
bookplate (Jo-Ann Scrap Essentials)
fibers (Making Memories, Fibers on the Fringe and Anchor)
label (Dymo)
unknown ribbon, flower, spiral clip
fonts Scrap Casual, Bradley Hand, CK Constitution, Adler, Angelina, Roddy, Papyrus and Architext

CHAPTER FIVE—JOURNEY

Santa Fe: A Journey To the "City Different"
Elizabeth Dillow | Colorado Springs, CO

album 8½ × 11 (Kolo)
stamps Architecture (Stampin' Up!)
rub-ons (Making Memories)
metal-rimmed tag (Making Memories)
jump ring (Making Memories)
paper clip (Making Memories)
unknown key, t-pin and acrylic paint
font Bernhard Modern BT Roman

3 Days
Sheila Doherty | Coeur d'Alene, ID

album 8 × 8 (Mrs. Grossman's)
application Adobe Illustrator (Adobe Systems)
patterned paper (KI Memories and American Crafts)

stickers alphabet (Making Memories)
ribbon (Offray)
metal stitched circles (Making Memories)
stamps (Making Memories)
unknown vellum
font Rockwell font

San Francisco
Cory Richardson-Lauve | Richmond, VA

album 8½ × 11 (Pioneer Photo Albums, Inc.)
application Adobe Photoshop Elements (Adobe Systems)
patterned paper (Carolee's Creations, Scrapbook Wizard and Paper Adventures)
stamps Jive Alphabet (All Night Media)
eyelets (Making Memories)
snaps (Making Memories)
fonts Marydale, My Handwriting (created on Internet at www.fontifier.com) Artiste 1, Times New Roman, Market, ITC Matisse, Arial and Curly Coryphaeus fonts

CHAPTER SIX—OTHER ALBUMS WE LOVED

Our Hawaiian Holiday
Amy Trask | Marina, CA

album 8½ × 11 (Pioneer Photo Albums, Inc.)
patterned paper (BasicGrey, Creative Imaginations, K&Company, American Traditional Designs, DieCuts with a View, Leisure Arts, Memories in the Making, Rocky Mountain Scrapbook Co., Provo Craft, Karen Foster Design, Rusty Pickle and NRN Designs)
brads (Making Memories)
eyelets (Making Memories)
stickers plumeria, hibiscus, surfboards and bamboo letter (Creative Imaginations), letters (BasicGrey)
stamps (Making Memories and Stampin' Up!)
stamping ink (Ranger Industries)
photo corners leather (Making Memories)
tags (Making Memories and BasicGrey)
bookplate (KI Memories)
bottle caps (Li'l Davis Designs)
chipboard letters (Li'l Davis Designs)
wood chips (Heidi Grace Designs)
twill tape (Pebbles, Inc.)
tags Scrabble, Nostalgiques typewriter letter and distressed tag (EK Success), shell tag (O'Scrap!)
die-cuts (Deluxe Designs)
unknown ribbon, flowers, starfish button, fabric
fonts Marcelle Script, Viner Hand, Lainie Day, Bodoni, Clarendon Condensed, Book Antiqua, B52, Stencil, CK Cursive, MA Sexy, Black Jack, Brody, Felt, Giraffe, CAC Shishoni Brush, Pushkin, Frazzle, Impact, and Hans Hand

I'm Not Cute, I'm Two
Julie Dominguez | Auburn, WA

album 8½ × 11 (Pioneer Photo Albums, Inc.)
applications Adobe Photoshop Elements 2 (Adobe Systems)
font Comic Sans

Our Family Favorites
Samantha VanArnhem | Olmsted Falls, OH

album spiral-bound (unknown)
patterned paper (SEI)
tags (SEI)
tabs (SEI)
brads (Making Memories)

Why a Son Needs a Dad
Sarah Little | Sugar Hill, GA

album 8 × 8 (Colorbök)
stamps Philadelphia lowercase foam (Making Memories)
fonts Script MT Bold and Onyx

Celebrate My Life
Tish Treadaway | Harrisburg, NC

album 12 × 12 Perfect Fit (Making Memories)
patterned paper (Making Memories, 7gypsies and Hearts & Crafts)
brads (Making Memories)
eyelets (Making Memories)
snaps (Making Memories)
fibers (Making Memories, On the Surface and Elegant Accents)
ribbon (Making Memories and Offray)
paperclips (Making Memories)
flowers (Making Memories)
metal charms (Making Memories)
frames (Making Memories)
buckles (Making Memories)
photo corners (Canson)
fonts Script MT Bold, CK Extra, CK Elegant, CK Cosmopolitan, Times New Roman, Two Peas Thrift Store, CBX Heber and Faith

March
Sherri Horton | Conway, AR

album 6 × 6 mini book (Making Memories)
brads white dragonfly (Accent Depot)
rub-ons (Making Memories)

In all my years as an editor, few projects have ever touched or inspired me as much as this one. I am deeply moved by the caring, commitment and creativity that have obviously gone into scrapbooking every heartfelt album you'll find in **Scrapbooks to Cherish.**

Our authors transformed life-defining details into heirloom albums by having the dedication, and in some cases the courage, to get it down on paper. I am impressed by the many rich and easily forgotten details that have been preserved in the telling of even the simplest of these stories.

I am also intrigued by the variety of original approaches the authors used to frame their albums. All of them are as unique as the lives and stories they chose to honor.

I hope you'll be as touched and inspired as I was. There's a story in your life that's waiting to be told. Memories only live forever if someone takes time to preserve them. That someone may be you.

Warmest regards,

Lynda Angelastro

Lynda Angelastro
Special Projects Editor
Simple Scrapbooks

The phone rang around 10:00 p.m.. Mr. Rosolie, the high school principal was on the phone. He said, "You're not going believe what just happened." Of course my heart dropped into my stomach and thought it was something bad. "What happened?" I said. "You're daughter was just named Prom Queen!" I shouted "WHAT? Katey?" Michael came running from upstairs and Dad thought something bad had happened until I yelled, "KATEY WAS JUST CROWNED PROM QUEEN!" Mr. Rosolie congratulated me and said, "She looks beautiful!" Karen Aughman, Katey's kindergarten teacher grabbed the phone was laughing and congratulating me. She said, "She looks gorgeous! I voted for her!" I was so excited for you. This was definitely a "Night to Remember"! We were thrilled for you!

Case Number: 00045

Date: 8/31/2004

The suspect was brought into custody this evening, and a positive identification given. The minor in question was apprehended at

147